# Table of Contents

# Executive Summary

Each year, Federal agencies invest billions of dollars in civil Earth observations. Through these investments, the U.S. government ensures that the Nation's decision makers, businesses, first-responders, farmers, and a wide array of other stakeholders have the information they need about climate and weather, disaster events, land-use change, ecosystem health, natural resources, and many other characteristics of the planet. Taken together, Earth observations provide the indispensable foundation for meeting the Federal Government's long-term sustainability objectives and advancing U.S. social, environmental, and economic well-being.

As the Nation's Earth-observation capacity has grown, however, so has the complexity of this endeavor. Today, U.S. Earth-observation efforts are distributed among more than 100 programs under the purview of Federal agencies and non-Federal entities that both produce and use these data.[1] The National Strategy for Civil Earth Observations, developed in response to congressional direction,[2] is designed to maximize interagency coordination, increase efficiency and efficacy of future Earth-observation efforts, and promote environmental and economic sustainability.

The National Strategy includes two main elements:

- A policy framework and method for Federal Government assessment of Earth observations (data and products derived from Earth-observing systems) that defines societal benefit areas, evaluates information products produced for those areas, identifies critical data streams that support those products, and prioritizes the observing systems on which those data streams depend, taking account of both present capabilities and anticipated needs and technologies.

- Data-management guidelines that advance data-management frameworks and improve information-delivery systems for Earth-observation data.

A third element—a National Plan for Civil Earth Observations, based on the results of the assessment and that takes fiscal and programmatic constraints into account—is to be published as a supplement to the President's budget for fiscal year (FY) 2014.

This National Strategy pertains to observations and data for civilian-use purposes. It strives toward openness and integration of data from Federal and non-Federal sources, including unclassified products derived from classified sources, while explicitly recognizing that certain sources of data may require greater oversight, protection, and potential restriction due to national-security, privacy, and confidentiality considerations.

The National Strategy provides a method of assessing Earth-observing systems by defined societal benefit areas—a key prerequisite to crafting a National Plan for Civil Earth Observations. This organization around benefit areas is designed to consider the relative impact of observations from multiple sources, as well as the need for measurement continuity for societal benefits that depend on sustained, long-term, and accurate measurements.

---

[1] Non-Federal entities encompass state, regional, local, and tribal governments; nongovernmental organizations; academia; citizen scientists; commercial firms; international organizations; and foreign governments.

[2] See Appendix A.

While Earth observations are typically produced for a specific purpose, they are often found to be useful for additional purposes not foreseen during the development of the observation system. Earth-observation data should be managed and preserved such that both anticipated and unanticipated users can find, evaluate, understand, and use the data in new ways. This National Strategy, therefore, sets out a comprehensive data-management framework as an integral element of current and future Earth-observation planning, to ensure effective and continuing access to Earth observations by the full range of potential users and beneficiaries.

The National Plan for Civil Earth Observations, once completed for FY 2014, is intended to be updated every 3 years to inform Federal investments in civil Earth-observation systems. This approach of routine assessment, improved data management, and coordinated planning is designed to enable stable, continuous, and coordinated Earth-observation capabilities for the benefit of society.

# 1. Overview and Policy Framework

## 1.1. Introduction

Federal investments in civil Earth observations provide critical societal benefits by enabling scientists, decision-makers, and citizens to advance the drivers of U.S. economic, social, and environmental well-being. Such investments allow the deployment of renewable energy technologies and other sustainable practices such as integrated water-resource management, coastal and marine planning, climate-adaptation strategies, and sustainable land use. Recent Earth-system science research has also revealed important new knowledge that results directly from closing gaps in critical time-series observations and improving observations of complex Earth-system processes, including human activity.

Without routine and comprehensive Earth observations, the Nation risks not having adequate information to respond to crises and to evaluate potentially harmful long-term trends. For example:

- During natural and human-induced disasters, both existing observational data and real-time monitoring are needed to develop effective response measures that mitigate loss of life and property.
- A lack of long-term and continuous observational data undermines the credibility of environmental data records.
- Sudden loss of, or unexpected data gaps in, routine observations can dramatically affect forecasting and modeling accuracy. This can contribute to poor decision-making with substantial economic and social costs. Certain data gaps are irreplaceable, inhibiting the ability to link past and future measurements.

As such, Earth observations provide the basic information necessary for meeting the Federal Government's long-term sustainability objectives, which include: (1) encouraging the use of sustainability science as a mechanism to integrate human and natural sciences, ecosystem science, ecosystem recovery and restoration work, land-use and watershed considerations, and related areas for environmental and natural resource R&D, policy, and management; and (2) supporting science and technology for sustainability to promote sustainable products, processes, and systems.

The myriad Earth observations made today are distributed among more than 100 programs under the purview of Federal agencies and non-Federal entities that both produce and use Earth-observation data.[3] The magnitude and complexity of Federal-agency investments in civil Earth-observation activities require a regular, coordinated effort to review, assess, and optimize those investments. Achieving a greater degree of interagency coordination will improve the efficiency and efficacy of future Earth-observation efforts and promote environmental and economic sustainability.

## 1.2. Definition of Earth Observations

For the purposes of this document, the term "Earth observations" refers to data and products derived from Earth-observing systems and surveys. "Observing systems" refers to one or more sensing elements that directly or indirectly collect observations of the Earth, measure environmental parameters, or survey biological or other Earth resources (land surface, biosphere, solid Earth, atmosphere, and

---

[3] Non-Federal entities encompass state, regional, local, and tribal governments; nongovernmental organizations; academia; citizen scientists; commercial firms; international organizations; and foreign governments.

oceans).[4] Sensing elements may be deployed as individual sensors or in constellations or networks, and may include instrumentation or human elements. Observing-system platforms may be mobile or fixed and are space-based, airborne, terrestrial, freshwater, or marine-based. Observing systems increasingly consist of integrated platforms that support remotely sensed, in-situ, and human observations.

## 1.3. Guidelines for the National Plan for Civil Earth Observations

In response to Congressional direction, the National Strategy for Civil Earth Observations establishes guidelines, processes, and criteria for the development of a National Plan for Civil Earth Observations to guide Federal investments in civil Earth-observation systems. The purpose of the plan will be to enable stable, continuous, and coordinated global Earth observation capabilities for the benefit of society. The National Plan will be informed by an assessment process for determining priorities, which will use an approach that explicitly links goals and strategies to resource availability and optimized allocations.[5]

The National Plan, targeted for initial publication for FY 2014, will be updated every 3 years to ensure it reflects revised observational requirements, new and improved technologies, domestic and international developments, and revised budget outlooks. A 10-year horizon will be considered for the first National Plan and in each update to incorporate the evolution of Earth-observing needs, assess near- and long-term information requirements, and identify methods to better integrate the U.S. portfolio of systems, networks, and platforms necessary to meet those requirements. This includes the data-management and information-delivery mechanisms integral to all Earth-observation systems. In addition, the National Strategy envisions close collaboration with the modeling community and the private sector to ensure that (1) observations are integrated with Earth-system models and that the observation needs of the modeling community are addressed, and (2) data-management practices are established in coordination with existing community (non-Federal) data standards, where applicable.

The National Plan will be developed in accord with the following principles:

- **Information for Societal Benefit**: Identify information requirements and measurements needed to maximize societal benefits, in the areas described in Section 1.4 of this National Strategy. Specific attention will be given to observation of complex Earth-system processes (including coupled human and natural systems); observational requirements for Earth-system models; and acquisition and timely delivery of requisite and relevant information to scientists, service providers, on-scene emergency coordinators, public and private decision-makers, and the public. See Appendix B for elaboration of the questions that inform societal benefit.

- **Integrated Portfolio Management**: Manage the Federal Government's Earth-observation investments as a prioritized portfolio that integrates within and across the areas described in Section 1.4; integrate information requirements and measurements; coordinate federally oper-ated systems, networks, platforms, and programs; identify reliance on non-federally operated systems; optimize investments among different platforms; and optimize and balance research-data collection with operational monitoring.

- **Federal Collaboration**: Promote and facilitate effective collaboration among diverse Federal Earth-observation activities, and clarify observing and associated life-cycle data-management responsibilities, including metrics for responsiveness and timeliness.

---

[4] Model outputs are generally excluded from this definition; however, some observing systems produce and record measures and observations that may require sensor models to process raw observations to a form in which they are exploitable.
[5] Such an approach is referred to as Integrated Resource Management.

- **Interoperable Systems and Access**: Advance the integration and harmonization of data at the sensor, platform, data-processing, and application levels to ensure that data are comparable independent of sensor, platform, and organization; promote a service-oriented, standards-based technical architecture to provide interfaces to Earth-observing systems and their associated data-management systems, ensuring that users can both find and visualize the data; establish a user-driven policy and architecture for access to and archiving of federally funded observations (or other data by agreement) to ensure that they are widely available and accessible in a timely, efficient, and user-friendly manner.

- **Domestic and International Partnerships**: Identify critical dependencies and successful partnerships with non-Federal observing networks and achieve a greater degree of interagency coordination to improve the efficiency, efficacy, and costs of leveraging the observation networks of non-Federal entities.[6] See Appendix C for details.

- **U.S. Technical and Management Leadership**: Advance U.S. technical leadership in measurement and monitoring technologies by investing in a range of research and development that supports Earth observations, including the development of technologies, sensors, applications, and alternative approaches to recognize, prioritize, and appropriately respond to emerging information needs.

- **National-Security Assets**: Increase the use of national-security assets for civil purposes, where appropriate and in coordination with the Civil Applications Committee. Take the availability of these data into account when planning new missions, while maintaining protections for national security, personal privacy, and civil liberties.[7]

## 1.4. Observations and Information to Benefit Society

This Strategy establishes a process to evaluate Earth-observing systems based on the information products and data streams they support in defined societal benefit areas (SBAs). This approach was adopted by the National Science and Technology Council Committee on Environment, Natural Resources, and Sustainability in February of 2012, is consistent with the Federal Government's sustainability objectives, and aligns with international agreements and prior interagency work in this arena.[8] The first National Plan for Civil Earth Observations will be organized around 12 SBAs (listed alphabetically) and the reference measurements that underpin them:

- **Agriculture and Forestry**: Supporting sustainable agriculture and forestry.
- **Biodiversity**: Understanding and conserving biodiversity.

---

[6] Increasingly, Federal Agencies are relying on observing systems that are obtained in partnership with other entities through co-funding, leveraging, purchase arrangements ("data buys"), and other agreements to provide mutually beneficial Earth observation activities. These systems are often maintained by multiple funding sources and operated by non-Federal entities (domestic and international), either in cooperation with Federal Agencies or independently. Partnership arrangements are particularly common for Earth-observing satellites and other large-scale sensing and observing networks and infrastructure

[7] National security requirements and considerations are not covered by this strategy, though the use of national security assets for civil purposes is included. The Civil Applications Committee is an interagency committee that coordinates and oversees the Federal civil use of classified collections

[8] Group on Earth Observations, Global Earth Observation System of Systems (GEOSS): 10 Year Implementation Plan Reference Document, 2005, www.earthobservations.org/documents/10-Year%20Plan%20Reference%20Document.pdf; Interagency Working Group on Earth Observations, Strategic Plan for the U.S. Integrated Earth Observation System, NSTC Committee on Environment and Natural Resources, 2005, www.whitehouse.gov/sites/default/files/microsites/ostp/eocstrategic_plan.pdf

- **Climate**: Understanding, assessing, predicting, mitigating, and adapting to climate variability and related global change.
- **Disasters**: Reducing loss of life, property, and ecosystem damage from natural and human-induced disasters.
- **Ecosystems (Terrestrial and Freshwater)**: Improving the management and protection of terrestrial and freshwater ecosystems.
- **Energy and Mineral Resources**: Improving the identification and management of energy and mineral resources.
- **Human Health**: Understanding environmental factors affecting human health and well-being.
- **Ocean and Coastal Resources and Ecosystems**: Understanding and protecting ocean, coastal, and Great Lakes populations and resources, including fisheries, aquaculture, and marine ecosystems.
- **Space Weather**: Understanding, assessing, predicting, and mitigating the effects of space weather on technological systems, including satellites, power grids, communications, and navigation.
- **Transportation**: Improving the safety and efficiency of all modes of transportation, including air, highway, railway, and marine.
- **Water Resources**: Improving water resource management through better understanding and monitoring of the water cycle.
- **Weather**: Improving weather information, forecasting, and warning.
- **Reference Measurements**: Improving reference measurements—the underpinnings of all the SBAs—such as geodesy, bathymetry, topography, geolocation, and the fundamental measurement systems and standards supporting them.

These SBAs are interconnected and include scientific research, economic activities, and environmental and social domains. Multiple SBAs share observational requirements, and societal benefits accrue from Earth observations that inform scientific research, policy, and decision-making. Earth observations also support critical government functions, such as the continuity of national government and the protection of life and property. The SBAs are described in greater detail in Appendix B.

# 2. Assessment Method and Plan Development

## 2.1. Introduction

This chapter describes the assessment method for the development of a National Plan for Civil Earth Observations and subsequent triennial updates. The overall process is designed to be accomplished in two phases:

- **Phase 1: Portfolio Assessment**. The foundational element for the National Plan is an internal assessment of existing and planned observing systems in providing environmental observations to benefit society across the SBAs. The assessment evaluates the current portfolio and makes recommendations, for internal Federal use, concerning continuity, fulfillment, and advancement of required measurements over a 10-year planning period,[9] taking account of existing capabilities and anticipated needs and technologies.

- **Phase 2: National Plan for Civil Earth Observations**. Using the portfolio assessment, the Executive Office of the President (EOP), in close coordination with agency leadership, will develop a cross-agency National Plan consistent with the President's budget for specific Earth observation systems, platforms, and networks. This plan will be published as a supplement to the President's budget.

## 2.2. Phase 1: Portfolio Assessment

The portfolio assessment process is designed to review the impact of observations from multiple sources. The process examines measurement continuity for societal benefits that depend on sustained, long-term, and accurate measurements.

The first portfolio assessment was carried out in 2012 by an interagency Assessment Working Group appointed by the NEO Task Force, supported by expert teams for each societal benefit area to aid the EOP in establishing Earth observation priorities for the Nation. In evaluating existing systems and making recommendations for the future, the assessment process considered, among other criteria, the following characteristics of observing systems:

- Impact on a single SBA or multiple SBAs.
- Ability to complement other observational systems, including international, commercial, civil, and non-civil systems.
- Degree of risk, including readiness (technical, resources, people).
- Mitigation of risk and strategic redundancy (backup of other critical systems).

The Assessment Working Group began by refining the assessment method and prioritization criteria presented in this National Strategy. The Working Group drew from experts who are familiar with the use of remote sensing, in-situ, and other Earth observation techniques. The group also drew on current and potential users who focus on the development of decision-essential science and tools using the data.

---

[9] For the purposes of the assessment, Earth-observing systems were addressed primarily at the program level. Further, consideration of Earth observation systems with primary dependency on human Earth observation sensing elements were limited to those programs that regularly and systematically collect observations and measures to produce periodically required data that are vital to an agency's mission.

## 2.2.1. SBA Assessment Teams

To ensure that the right expertise was available and engaged throughout the process, technical experts were identified to lead and support assessment teams for each SBA. The Assessment Working Group worked with subcommittees of the National Science and Technology Council's (NSTC) Committee on Environmental, Natural Resources, and Sustainability (CENRS) to identify lead and contributing experts for each team. The Assessment Working Group provided centralized guidance and oversight to ensure that each of the SBA assessments were completed to the same level of detail and that each team applies the assessment criteria uniformly across the SBAs.

## 2.2.2. SBA Assessment Process

The SBA assessment teams used the process outlined below to complete an assessment and evaluate the impact of observing on each of the SBAs.

1. *Identification and Definition of SBA Subareas.* SBAs transcend individual agency needs and mandates, and describe broad societal, scientific, and economic goals. Because SBAs are broad, the first step was to identify major subareas within each SBA. This facilitated broad coverage as well as provided a framework for identifying the needed expertise.

2. *Identification of Key Objectives.* SBA teams identified key objectives for each subarea. Key objectives are those activities, products, services, or desired end states which rely in whole or in part on Earth-observation data to provide societal benefit. The objectives clearly identified what is being achieved using Earth observations.

3. *Identification of the Current Observing System Portfolio.* SBA teams identified data sources (observing systems providing direct observations) and tools (models, products, etc.) that are required to achieve the key objectives. Where products or models were identified, an additional step was necessary to determine the observing systems providing data to the model or used to produce the product. This value chain analysis was repeated until all observing system inputs supporting the objective are identified (see Figure 1). The final result is the list of observing systems currently contributing to achieving benefits in the 12 SBAs plus the reference measurements that underpin each.

4. *Assessment of Current Observing System Portfolio.* The Assessment Working Group will provided standardized guidance to the SBA teams, defining the method for determining the relative impact and performance of the observing system portfolio identified in Step 3. The method also included an evaluation of the current performance level for each objective, sub-area and SBA, which formed the baseline for evaluating and prioritizing gaps in step 5. The result of this step was an impact-ranking of the current portfolio of observing systems.

5. *Development of Recommendations for the National Plan for Civil Earth Observations.* Starting with the impact ranking, the SBA teams developed narrative recommendations, described in terms of maintaining continuity, mitigating risks and gaps, and identifying opportunities to capitalize on new or improved technologies that add capability, replace existing capabilities with more efficient cost-effective methods, plan for long-term data-set development, and leverage partnerships.

16

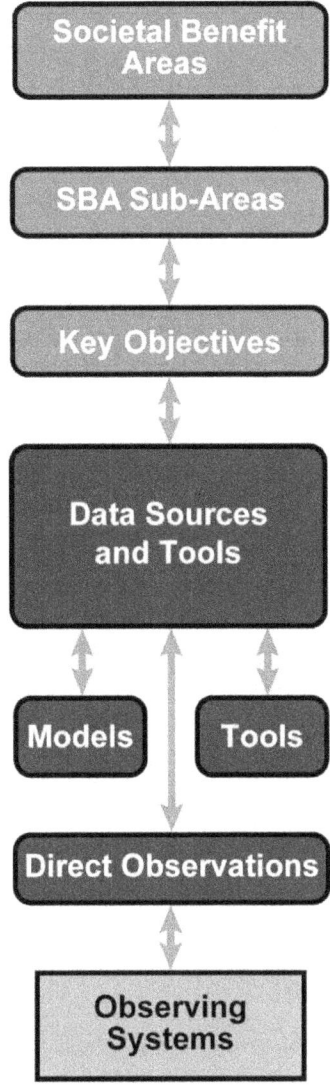

Figure 1: Value chain analysis

### 2.2.3. Integrated Assessment across SBAs

Once the individual SBA assessments were completed, the final activity in Phase 1 was for the Assessment Working Group to identify priorities for observational technologies and capabilities according to their contribution to measurement needs over the long-term planning horizon. The results of this assessment were provided as internal, deliberative input to the EOP for the formulation of the National Plan for Civil Earth Observations.

## 2.3. Phase 2: National Plan for Civil Earth Observations

The second phase is the development of the National Plan for Civil Earth Observations, which will be informed by the internal assessment as well as other external sources, such as the many reports of the National Academies relating to Earth observations. The National Plan will be published as a supplement to the President's budget. Building on the guidelines outlined in Section 1.3, the plan will take into account the following major considerations:

- **Coordinating Earth Observations from Space:** Given the large Federal investment in Earth observation satellite development and operation, strengthened planning about the requirements for space-based observation is necessary, as is investigating alternative technologies and approaches to meeting these requirements. In accordance with congressional direction, specific attention will be given to the development of a plan for sustained climate measurements from space.

- **Sustaining Long-Term Observations:** The National Plan will consider issues and options concerning the sustainability of civil Earth observations from demonstration and research programs, on all platforms, to long-term data-acquisition programs. (See Chapter 3 for more detail).

- **Delivering Integrated Information:** The Nation's investment in data-management and information-delivery systems is an integral part of the National Earth observation infrastructure. This National Strategy respects the "presumption of openness" called for in the 2009 Open Government Directive. Full, open, and timely sharing and exchange of data, products, and services through machine-readable formats and Application Programming Interfaces (APIs) will enable users to effectively and rapidly transform data into useful information products for society. The development of widely accepted standards, principles, and guidelines for data management, dissemination, and quality will encourage and facilitate the integration of diverse U.S. Earth observations for the benefit of society, and it will contribute to existing and coordination efforts. This National Strategy adheres to the principle that access to data-managed or paid for using Federal funds should be open to the public as soon as possible after collection, in a nondiscriminatory manner, and generally free of charge. Agencies may set user charges in a manner consistent with Office of Management and Budget (OMB) Circular A-130.[10]

- **Affordability:** Cost considerations, including development, deployment, operations, and maintenance costs year and integrated costs of missions and programs over multiple years.

- **Identifying Common Needs and Sharing Resources:** Data needs across SBAs will be compared to identify common requirements and opportunities to share observing and data-management systems resources.

- **Interdependency of Federal and Non-Federal Observing Systems:** Observational networks funded in part by the Federal Government may also contain components owned by non-Federal entities. In some cases, these systems may be more cost effective than wholly Federal observational networks, but they can also require complex funding and management arrangements, which involve risk because quality control and continuation of these observations is not under the direct control of the Federal Government. Governance of these systems must be accomplished through coordinated policies for inventory control, data ownership and sharing, and public-private partnerships. Similarly, observational networks that are supported by more than one agency (e.g., ground-based measurements needed to support space-based measurements) pose special challenges to continuity and will need to be coordinated.

- **Engaging the Private Sector and the Public:** Mechanisms for engaging industry, non-governmental organizations, and other stakeholders in Earth observation will be developed or

---

[10] Office of Management and Budget. Circular A-130, Revised (Transmittal Memorandum No. 4), 2000, www.whitehouse.gov/sites/default/files/omb/circulars/a130/a130trans4.pdf.

enhanced to take advantage of the competencies and contributions of stakeholders and the potential benefits of increased U.S. competitiveness in the private sector.

- **Improving User Engagement:** Mechanisms for engaging user communities will be developed to cultivate wider application and use of Earth observations.

- **Leveraging National Security Assets:** Existing mechanisms for increasing the use of national security assets for civil purposes will be strengthened, while maintaining protections for national security, personal privacy, and civil liberties.

Building on the assessment of Earth observation systems and needs developed in Phase 1, the Executive Office of the President (EOP), in close coordination with agency leadership, will develop the National Plan. Consistent with congressional direction, the National Plan will address agency roles and responsibilities in Earth observations and will take account of known budgetary and programmatic constraints.

The EOP will complete a first draft of the National Plan for Civil Earth Observations. The final draft will be reviewed by CENRS and published by the EOP as a supplement to the President's FY 2014 Budget. As required by Congress, the plan will be updated every 3 years, including a process for independent external advisory input.

# 3. Data Management and Delivery

## 3.1. Introduction

This chapter presents a framework for the delivery, quality, and preservation of Earth-observation data, including data-management principles, guidance, approaches, architectural considerations, standardization, and evaluation. This framework incorporates concepts and recommendations from recent studies by the National Research Council, the Interagency Working Group on Digital Data (IWGDD), the United States Group on Earth Observations (USGEO), the United States Chief Information Officer, the strategic plans of the participating agencies, and Open Government initiatives such as Data.gov.[11]

While Earth observations are typically produced for a specific purpose, they are often found to be useful for additional purposes not foreseen during the development of the observation system. It is important that Earth-observation data be managed and preserved such that both anticipated and unanticipated users can find, evaluate, understand, and utilize the data in new ways. The wide range of scientific and observation efforts of Federal agencies, and the resulting magnitude of data collections and diversity of data types, requires an approach that is broadly applicable yet able to be tailored to particular needs. Specifically, the National Plan will take into account the many observation and data-management initiatives currently under development (see textbox on the following page).

This document sets out a comprehensive data-management framework of transparent, evolvable, extensible policies and associated management and organizational structures to provide effective and continuing access to Earth observations. This framework sets expectations and requirements for Federal agencies involved in the collection, processing, stewardship, and dissemination of Earth-observation data. The data policies of entities outside the Federal Government are beyond the scope of this document. The framework described here, however, applies to the use of all data by Federal agencies, regardless of source. The goal is to (1) maximize the likelihood that Earth observations are available and disseminated in a timely and usable manner, (2) facilitate the transformation of observations into useful information through the use of open, machine readable-formats and APIs, and (3) encourage the development and use of uniform tools and practices across Federal agencies for the handling of Earth-observation data to increase interoperability. The framework should guide and inform the development and implementation of agency- and program-specific data-management plans.

Toward those ends, Federal agencies should collect, maintain, disseminate, and preserve Earth observations so that the resulting data and products can be readily shared with other Federal agencies and non-Federal users, promoting data integration between sources. Agencies should ensure that Earth-observation data and products are included on agency record schedules that have been approved by the appropriate authorities.[12] These activities will adhere to appropriate standards and be conducted in accordance with existing regulations.

---

[11] Committee on Archiving and Accessing Environmental and Geospatial Data at NOAA, Environmental Data Management at NOAA: Archiving, Stewardship and Access, National Research Council, 2007, www.nap.edu/catalog. php?record_id=12017; OSTP Interagency Working Group on Digital Data, Harnessing the Power of Digital Data: Taking the Next Step, 2011; and United States Group on Earth Observations, Exchanging Data for Societal Benefit: An IEOS Web Services Architecture, 2008; U.S. Chief Information Officer, 25 Point Implementation Plan to Reform Federal Information Technology Management, 2010, www.cio.gov/documents/25-Point-Implementation-Plan-to-Reform-Federal%20IT.pdf.

[12] A record schedule is an agency's official policy on how long to retain agency records and how to dispose of them.

**Data and Information Management Initiatives**

*A comprehensive data-management framework, as outlined in this strategy, will be necessary to support the following initiatives, among others:*

**GCIS:** The Global Change Information System (GCIS) has the immediate priority of meeting the needs of the National Climate Assessment (NCA). The goal of the GCIS will be to integrate multiple agency components into an interagency system that allows easy access to usable climate services.
**Ocean.data.gov:** Created by the National Ocean Council to support Coastal and Marine Spatial Planning.
**U.S. IOOS DMAC:** The Data Management and Communications (DMAC) subsystem of the IOOS is overseen by the Subcommittee on Ocean Science and Technology's (SOST) Integrated Ocean Observations Committee.
**EcoINFORMA:** A recommendation by the President's Council of Advisors on Science and Technology (PCAST) was for an Ecoinformatics-based Open Resources and Machine Accessibility initiative to better enable use of bioinformatics data.
**Biodiversity Monitoring:** PCAST also recommended a data gaps and priorities assessment of Federal and regional ecological monitoring systems, accompanied by integrating existing monitoring networks.
**Data.gov and OpenEI:** Energy resource and consumption datasets, tools, and applications in open government platforms, such as Data.gov/Energy and OpenEI.org, already aid in identifying climate change mitigation opportunities.
**WaterML:** Water Markup Language (ML) is an informatics initiative of the CENRS Subcommittee on Water Availability and Quality that provides a systematic way to access water information from point observation sites.
**LCA database:** The Life Cycle Assessment (LCA) database is the United States Department of Agriculture's new initiative to incorporate environmental and crop data into a life cycle assessment of manufactured products and other goods and services.
**DOI Initiatives:** Information compiled and collected through the Landscape Conservation Cooperatives, and Climate Science Centers established under the DOI's climate change science initiative, will be part of a national and, ultimately, international network.
**OFCM:** The Office of the Federal Coordinator for Meteorology (OFCM) Committee for Integrated Observing System coordinates weather and climate observing networks to create a *network of networks.*


All of these information initiatives are interlinked and comport with Data.gov activities under the Open Government Initiative, and the Digital Government Strategy, including the merger of the Federal Geographic Data Committee's Geospatial OneStop into Data.gov.

Federal agencies should continue efforts to encourage data openness, data sharing, and increased data access in the international system, in particular by advancing the data sharing principles of the Global Earth Observation System of Systems (GEOSS).[13]

The following definitions apply to the key concepts in this chapter:

- **Data:** For the purposes of this discussion, we use the terms "data" and "Earth observations" interchangeably to mean geo-referenced digital information about Earth, including the observations, metadata,[14] imagery, derived products, data-processing algorithms (including computer source code and its documentation), and forecasts and analyses produced by computer models. Non-digital data, published papers, preserved geological or biological samples, or other media that have not been digitized are not included in this definition and are outside the scope of this chapter.

- **Data-Management Framework:** The policies, requirements, activities, and technical considerations relevant to data produced or handled by an agency or program.

- **Data Life Cycle:** All the activities that affect data before and during its lifetime, including planning for and producing, managing, disseminating, using, and disposing of the data.[15]

- **Data-Management Life-Cycle Process:** An approach to managing the flow of an information system's data throughout the life cycle of the data.

- **Data Durability:** Durable data are those that are managed to ensure lasting value and usability for both their original purpose and new applications, thus providing maximum utility for scientific understanding, decision-making processes, and public access today and in the future.

- **Data Delivery**: The delivery or hosting of Earth observations so that the widest possible number of users may access the data, agnostic of platform. The development of specific information service delivery mechanisms, such as portals, for specific communities is beyond the scope of this document.

The concepts in this National Strategy pertain to data for civilian-use purposes; they reflect the goal of greater openness and integration of data from Federal and non-Federal sources, including unclassified derived products from classified sources. This Strategy explicitly recognizes that certain sources of data may require greater oversight, protection, and potential restriction due to national security, privacy, and confidentiality considerations.

---

[13] . See Section 5.4, "Data Sharing" of Group on Earth Observations, "Global Earth Observation System of Systems (GEOSS): 10 Year Implementation Plan," 2005. http://www.earthobservations.org/documents/10-Year%20Implementation%20Plan.pdf.

[14] More information on metadata can be found in Annex D.

[15] The data life cycle discussed in this chapter should not be confused with the concept of life cycle analysis, which is a technique to assess environmental impacts associated with all the stages of a product's development and use from raw material through disposal.

## 3.2. Data-Management Framework

The data-management framework is founded on the core concept of the data life cycle, defined below, and several crosscutting themes, including principles, guidance, architecture, standards, and evaluation, which are also discussed below. It is important to note that the crosscutting themes can be applied to the management of all data sets, and there are also separate lifecycles for each data set.

### 3.2.1. Data Life Cycle

The core of the data-management framework is the *data life cycle*, which can be divided into three activities as shown in Figure 2:

- Planning and production, which includes all activities up to, and including, the moment that observations are collected.
- Data management, which includes all activities related to collecting, storing, verifying, documenting, advertising, distributing, disposal, and preserving the data.
- Usage, which includes all activities performed by the consumer of the data.

These data life cycle activities are discussed in greater detail in Appendix D.

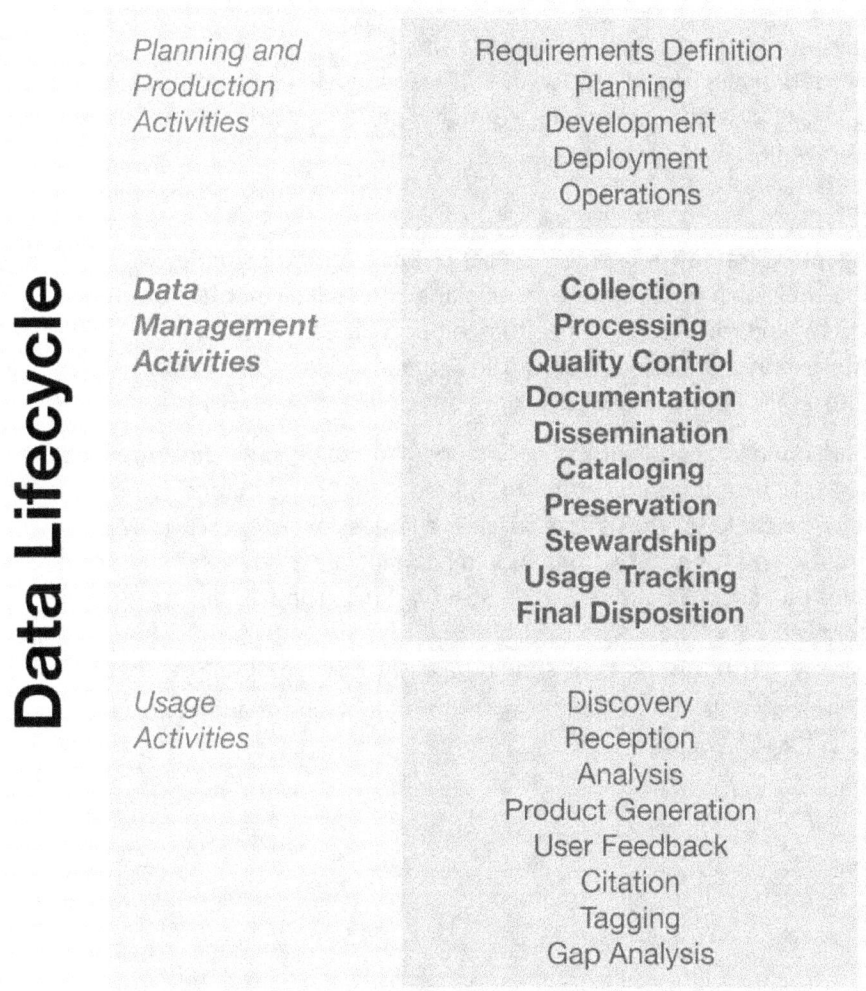

**Figure 2: Activities in the data life cycle. Data-management activities, emphasized in this chapter, are shown in bold.**

A life-cycle data-management process promotes durability of data; ensures that users are able to easily discover and access data, understand their context, and use them both for their intended purpose and in novel ways to aid research and decision-making; and ensures the durability of any derived data by linking their context to that of the original data upon which they are based.

Data life cycle process steps are interdependent. For example, inadequate documentation at an early stage can prevent later use; generating products from original data may yield new derived data that must also be collected and managed; and user feedback regarding data may change or augment documentation relating to the data. Because data may go through multiple cycles of use and reuse by different entities for different purposes, effective management of each step and coordination across steps in the life cycle are required to ensure that data are preserved and can be accessed and used efficiently and for new applications.

In the proposed process, data and associated metadata are acquired and incorporated into Federal data archives, where the data are evaluated and validated, supplemental data may be added, and data and data sets are maintained through a stewardship process that may involve both Federal experts and users. These data may further be integrated into new or enhanced data sets or products that reside in the repository or archive for use. Data and products, as well as metadata and standards, should be continually reviewed and improved throughout the data-management life cycle.

The resulting system must provide consistent, efficient, open, and nondiscriminatory access across multiple Federal data archives and repositories. These guidelines must also take into account access to both new and legacy systems, preserving compatibility when possible to allow users access to, and discovery of, archived Earth observations.

### 3.2.2. Principles

The data-management framework provides a set of basic principles under which relevant Federal agencies will develop their own data-management plans and requirements. The principles are summarized and explained here, and relevant guidance that supports these principles is provided in later sections of the chapter. These principles are elaborated in Appendix D and are in accordance with United States Global Change Research Program (USGCRP) data principles (see Annex B).

- **Full and open access:** Earth observations should be fully and openly available to all users promptly, in a nondiscriminatory and platform-agnostic manner, and generally free of charge wherever possible. Agencies may set user charges consistent with OMB Circular A-130.
- **Preservation:** Earth observations should be managed as an asset and preserved for future use.
- **Information data quality:** Earth observations should be of known quality and fully documented.
- **Ease of use:** Earth observations should be easily discoverable, searchable, and accessible online using interoperable services and standardized, machine-readable formats that encourage the broadest possible use.

These principles apply to all Federal Earth observations, with case-by-case exceptions for particular data sets.

### 3.2.3. Guidance

All civilian Federal agencies that produce or manage Earth observations or related data should:

- Establish a publicly available open data policy and a supporting data-management approach that addresses all aspects of the data life cycle, including open publishing of data, and metadata and quality-assurance management.
- Solicit and acknowledge stakeholder requirements and feedback with an understanding of the data use in advancing environmental, economic, and societal sustainability.
- Make data and services available in ways that support a web-based, service-oriented architecture (SOA) approach as described in Exchanging Data for Societal Benefit: An IEOS Web Services Architecture (USGEO 2008).[16][20]
- Provide nondiscriminatory data access and dissemination to interested users.
- Determine what data require long-term preservation and how preservation will be accomplished in conjunction with National Archives and Records Administration. Whenever possible, coordinate observation and data-management systems with appropriate archives early in the life cycle.
- Support data durability by providing assured delivery to an archive, secure storage, secondary offsite storage, and ongoing data stewardship to ensure continued accessibility and readability.
- Implement interactive discovery and access mechanisms for data and web services compatible with those of other agencies, including Data.gov and GEOSS, and other non-Federal users.
- Enable integration and interoperability with broadly used data-analysis software and decision-support tools. Demonstrate these approaches for derived products and delivery.
- Acknowledge that data-management and information delivery services are fundamental, integral aspects of any Earth observation endeavor, and provide sufficient resources in agency funding submissions for data-management and information delivery.

The data-management framework does not impose a one-size-fits-all plan. Given the wide variety of agency missions and data types, it is not reasonable to expect that a single plan can apply to multiple agencies or even throughout a single agency. Agencies have the freedom to create flexible approaches or plans that conform to specific operational needs of each program or data set, account for Earth observations through their life cycles, and allow for special cases. Agencies should develop capacity to assist in developing life-cycle data-management plans in accordance with the principles laid out in this framework.

In addition to agency activities, robust, focused, and sustained interagency coordination is needed to foster compatibility of data and systems from different agencies; to reduce costs by sharing software, standards, and best practices; to pool resources in acquisition of data-management technology or enhancements; and to avoid duplicative or conflicting methods and acquisitions.

### 3.2.4. Architecture

Earth-observation data exist in and are used across a number of heterogeneous platforms managed by multiple independent operators. These diverse systems cannot be subsumed into any single master system, but can be harmonized and connected through the use of interoperability standards and open publishing of data. Federal agencies should pursue an information system-of-systems approach to

---

[16] United States Group on Earth Observations, *Exchanging Data for Societal Benefit: An IEOS Web Services Architecture*, 2008, usgeo.gov/images/usgeomain/exchangingdataforsocietalbenefit.pdf

leverage and harmonize multiple legacy, modern, and future component systems that have evolved separately and are managed independently. An Earth observation information system of systems is a collection of agency- or project-specific information systems that are loosely coupled to deliver information and services to users while enabling each agency or program to remain the steward of its own information. This approach is enabled by the Internet and is the practical basis of GEOSS, referenced in Chapter 1.

A fundamental requirement of this approach is interoperability: "the ability of two or more systems or components to exchange information and to use the information that has been exchanged."[17] Interoperability enables diverse data, tools, systems, and archives to be combined without writing custom software to handle every data link. Interoperability issues in the system-of-systems approach are accommodated through the implementation of SOA as described in *Exchanging Data for Societal Benefit: An IEOS Web Services Architecture* (USGEO 2008), which provides a suite of loosely coupled interoperable services that are available over a network and can be used across systems and platforms. Interoperability can be applied at multiple levels, including data formats and content, metadata formats and content, data access interfaces, communication networks, and power and data connections for sensor systems. To optimize interoperability, Federal agencies and relevant stakeholder communities should coordinate standards, protocols, and standard vocabulary, as well as the planning and implementing of Earth observations systems, architectures, and repositories in the framework of an integrated data-management life-cycle process. To enable participation in a true system of systems, the documentation of these baseline implementation details—data content, data dictionary, protocols, schema, and formats—must be included in the metadata.

### 3.2.5. Standards

Standards are common rules, conditions, guidelines, or characteristics for data and related processes, technology, and organization. The broad use of a small set of common data, metadata, and protocol standards across Federal agencies (and international standards where possible) for data development, documentation, and exchange enhances the utility of Earth observations, decreases the cost of using the data, and helps Federal agencies avoid redundancies and waste.

Different types of standards are applicable to various aspects of the data life cycle, including standards for data quality,[18] metadata standards that specify the content and structure of documentation about a data set, and interoperability standards that specify the content and structure of the digital data and how services will interact. The use of existing national and international data, metadata, and protocol standards is recommended. Because such standards are often general-purpose and require specialization for specific data types, agencies are encouraged to publish the conventions, profiles, and examples they adopt to make these standards more applicable to their data. Collaboration among and within agencies is encouraged to adopt common conventions for using existing standards to maximize compatibility.

Guidance regarding standards for different activities in the data life cycle is provided in the next section. Different communities involved in the acquisition, processing, management, and use of Earth observations have developed different standards for handling data. Through the development of the

---

[17] Institute of Electrical and Electronics Engineers, *IEEE Standard Computer Dictionary: A Compilation of IEEE Standard Computer Glossaries*, New York, NY: 1990.

[18] In this document "data quality" references international standards approaches such as ISO 17025 that include traceability to the International System of Units (SI), the need for measurement uncertainty analysis, and the validation and verification of measurements.

National Plan and triennial review process, these diverse standards should be harmonized where possible and new community-based standards developed where there is a convergence of interest.

### 3.2.6. Evaluation

Agencies should evaluate the searchability, usability, openness, and utility of their data on an ongoing basis, to determine whether they are being used for intended and unanticipated purposes; whether their use has led to positive outcomes (e.g., improved forecasts, reduced costs, and lives saved); and whether the resources required to support data distribution, use, and preservation have increased or decreased as a result of adopting a more systematic approach to data management.

## 3.3. Data Innovations

Agencies should actively promote innovative uses of Earth-observation data. The America COMPETES Act authorizes the use of creative techniques such as challenges and contests to spur innovations that leverage Federal resources, including data.[19] In a resource-constrained environment that demands greater returns on Earth-observing investments, data and software oriented challenges can be particularly effective mechanisms for accelerating innovation and stimulating the creation of new capabilities that bring broad benefits. Most recently, in April 2012, NASA conducted the first International Space Apps Challenge to "encourage scientists and concerned citizens…to create, build, and invent new solutions to address challenges of global importance." Such forms of targeted innovation encouragement can help to enrich the Earth-observation data ecosystem with new capabilities. Challenges can also be used to foster the development of new ideas for uses of Earth-observation data, leading to new insights regarding user requirements that can be factored into subsequent efforts.

---

[19] America COMPETES Act (Public Law 110–69), www.gpo.gov/fdsys/pkg/PLAW-110publ69/content-detail.html.

# Appendix A: Authorities

The National Earth Observations (NEO) Task Force was chartered in February 2011 under the NSTC CENRS. The NEO Task Force was charged with developing the foregoing Strategy, in response to Congressional direction to the Director of OSTP.[20] A December 2010 OSTP report to Congress outlined the Administration's plans for the NEO Task Force.[21] The NEO Task Force efforts build on the work of USGEO and other subcommittees of the CENRS. The following NSTC departments and agencies are represented on the NEO Task Force:

Department of Agriculture;

Department of Commerce (Co-Chair);

Department of Defense;

Department of Energy;

Department of Homeland Security;

Department of the Interior (Co-Chair);

Department of State;

Environmental Protection Agency;

National Aeronautics and Space Administration (Co-Chair);

National Science Foundation;

Office of the Director of National Intelligence;

Smithsonian Institution; and,

U.S. Agency for International Development.

> *The Director of OSTP shall establish a mechanism to ensure greater coordination of the research, operations, and activities relating to civilian Earth observation . . .* National Aeronautics and Space Administration Authorization Act of 2010 (Pub. L. No. 111-267, October 11, 2010)

The following organizations in the Executive Office of the President are also represented on the NEO Task Force:

Council on Environmental Quality;

Office of Management and Budget; and,

Office of Science and Technology Policy (Co-Chair).

---

[20] Congressional direction for this activity is found in language from the National Aeronautics and Space Administration Authorization Act of 2010 (Public Law 111–267): SEC. 702. INTERAGENCY COLLABORATION IMPLEMENTATION APPROACH. The Director of OSTP should establish a mechanism to ensure greater coordination of the research, operations, and activities relating to civilian Earth observation of those Agencies, including NASA, that have active programs that either contribute directly or indirectly to these areas. This mechanism should include the development of a strategic implementation plan that is updated at least every 3 years, and includes a process for external independent advisory input. This plan should include a description of the responsibilities of the various Agency roles in Earth observations, recommended cost-sharing and procurement arrangements between Agencies and other entities, including international arrangements, and a plan for ensuring the provision of sustained, long-term space-based climate observations. The Director should provide a report to Congress within 90 days after the date of enactment of this Act on the implementation plan for this mechanism.

[21] See Annex A.

The National Strategy set forth in this document outlines a process to identify, implement, and update national civil Earth observation priorities. The heart of the strategy is the development of a National Plan to guide the development, deployment, and maintenance of Earth-observing systems. As required by Congress, the plan will be updated triennially through a robust, repeatable process that ensures correspondence with changing national needs and scientific understanding. The National Plan and process will leverage advances in Earth-observing technologies both nationally and internationally and will also include external, independent advisory input.

In addition to serving the primary mission and essential functions of the U.S. Government that require Earth observations, the National Plan will support the objectives of the U.S. Global Change Research Program and serve as the foundation of the U.S. contribution to the GEOSS.[22] The plan will serve as the practical realization of the 2005 strategy for the national Integrated Earth Observation System (IEOS).[23] The plan will also support and align with relevant legislation and policies including, but not limited to, the Global Change Research Act of 1990; the Clean Air Act Amendments of 1990; the National Space Policy of 2010; the Arctic Region Policy of 2009; the National Policy for the Stewardship of the Ocean, Our Coasts, and the Great Lakes of 2010; and OMB Circular A-16, "Coordination of Geographic Information and Related Spatial Data Activities." Both the National Strategy and the National Plan will include guidelines to support transparency and open government in accordance with the Open Government Directive[24] and the America COMPETES Reauthorization Act of 2010.[25]

---

[22] Group on Earth Observations, *Global Earth Observation System of Systems (GEOSS): 10 Year Implementation Plan Reference Document*, 2005, www.earthobservations.org/documents/10-Year%20Plan%20Reference%20Document.pdf.

[23] Interagency Working Group on Earth Observations, *Strategic Plan for the U.S. Integrated Earth Observation System*, NSTC Committee on Environment and Natural Resources, 2005, www.whitehouse.gov/sites/default/files/microsites/ostp/eocstrategic_plan.pdf.

[24] Office of Management and Budget, *Open Government Directive*, 2009, www.whitehouse.gov/sites/default/files/omb/assets/memoranda_2010/m10-06.pdf.

[25] America COMPETES Reauthorization Act of 2010, (Public Law 111–358), www.gpo.gov/fdsys/pkg/PLAW-111publ358/pdf/PLAW-111publ358.pdf.

# Appendix B: Representative Questions by Societal Benefit Area

The SBAs introduced in Section 1.4 are described in greater detail below. The descriptions of the SBAs are accompanied by a set of questions developed by the NEO Task Force's Policy Team to serve as a point of departure for further discussion on key Earth observation requirements. These sample questions have been culled from past agency, interagency, and National Academies' reports, as well as new input from the agencies represented on the NEO Task Force Policy Team. The questions below are notional and not prescriptive.

## Agriculture and Forestry

In the agriculture sector, societal benefits accrue from measurements that can inform both short- and long-term decision making by farmers, ranchers, foresters, rangeland managers, researchers, commodity markets, and governments. By supporting the producers of renewable products, this SBA aids the ability of farmers and foresters to satisfy food, feed, fiber, inputs for biofuels, and forest product needs. Important information requirements include measurements to support (1) production decisions; (2) agricultural forecasting; and (3) greenhouse gas mitigation in the agriculture and forestry sectors; (4) verification and compliance monitoring for crop insurance; and (5) crop-production monitoring to support international food security for timely famine and disaster relief. Improved data and information flow in these areas can contribute to (1) early warning systems for crop yield shortfalls and pest outbreaks; (2) understanding food, feed, forest products, and fiber needs in the context of expanding population and changing climate and biophysical resources; and (3) prevent degradation and desertification resulting from agricultural, deforestation, and grazing practices. Achieving these and other results requires effective national, regional, and local Earth observations of agriculture, rangelands, and forestry combined with comprehensive socioeconomic data at the local and regional scale. Key questions include the following:

- How can we effectively and continually monitor domestic and foreign yearly yields and harvests of food and fiber production at field, local, regional, and global scales?
- What systems are needed to develop timely feedback mechanisms at a local parcel level for within-season crop-production progress and early notification of warning factors, including pests, pathogens, water deficits, and nutrient deficiencies to enable adaptive management of agricultural production?
- How can we detect indicators of landscape health to aid in protecting crop lands, rangelands, grazing areas, and forests from degradation and desertification? How can we best measure soil erosion from wind and water to inform the understanding of tipping points for significant degradation? How can we measure land changes after natural disasters such as floods?
- In what ways are agriculture, forestry, and natural resources affected by invasive species, including plants, animals, insects, and diseases, and how can we detect and monitor the spread of disease in a timely, systematic, and synoptic manner to better derive global production from year to year? How can we track the effectiveness of remediation?

- How can we detect the effects of agro-terrorism (e.g., plant and animal diseases and waterborne pathogens), rapidly differentiate intentional infections from natural causes, and monitor progress of remediation?
- How do we monitor and manage land- and water-use competition for food and fiber production, alternative fuel sources, and urban and suburban development?
- How do we mitigate the impacts of climate change on agriculture and forestry?
- How can we detect and measure landscape factors relevant to compliance with agreements between landowners/operators and Federal and state agencies (e.g., conservations and farm programs, easements, timber sales, carbon conservation practices, and range management)? How can we monitor greenhouse gas flows from agriculture and managed forests at the parcel/field level?
- What systems are needed to detect and quantify the impact and speed of recovery from episodic catastrophic events such as drought, flood, hurricanes, tornadoes, earthquakes, and wildfires?
- How can we better monitor impacts of drought at field to county scales, to ensure equitable distribution of crop loss compensation?
- How can we effectively monitor and quantify land-use/land-cover change pertaining to agriculture and forestry, such as loss of agricultural land due to factors such as urbanization, desertification, etc.?
- How do we measure drought and characterize historical and pre-historical patterns of forest fires, including the systematic study and dating of scars in trees caused by forest fires? The patterns of natural wild-land fires (i.e., those that are unrelated to human activity) are a key baseline to maintaining the long-term health of natural vegetation, particularly in the southwestern United States.
- How do we effectively monitor and quantify the extent to which increases in insect, disease, and fire disturbance affect the biophysical characteristics of forests and affect the social and economic vales associated with forests?
- What is the former trends and current capacity of developed lands to sustain introduction of new crop variety or species with greater yield?
- Where do productive growth patterns appear to offer reusable elements or composites?
- How do cultural land use activities present opportunities for economic change on the margin or edge, within the network, or at the nodes?

## Biodiversity

This SBA addresses genetic, species, and ecosystem-level biodiversity. Monitoring for biodiversity supports strategic conservation decisions that promote balance within the ecosystems that humans depend on for their long-term well-being. This SBA provides information on the condition, extent, and diversity of ecosystems; distribution and health of species; and genetic diversity in key populations. Biodiversity measurements are important in both marine and terrestrial systems. Key questions include the following:

- What species exist, and where? Can we use remote sensing to support sustainable ecosystems enabling biodiversity preservation? How do we detect (1) native, intact communities of species of interest; (2) exotic species; and (3) regions of high species diversity?
- How do we identify the rates and geospatial characteristics of genetic variation in wild organisms? How will this help in determining spread of disease, loss of biodiversity, use of new biotechnology, and increases for global production while protecting biodiversity?

31

- What can biodiversity trends among widespread species tell us about how the environment around us is changing and about the sustainability of human land and ocean use at a broad scale?
- How do human activities (e.g., resource utilization, structures, disturbances, discharges, and runoff) affect biodiversity and patterns of distribution and movement of organisms?
- What can trends among the rare and threatened species tell us about localized extinction processes and about the efficacy of conservation actions at a local scale?
- What monitoring standards and sampling schemes are needed to enable non-specialists to contribute to rigorous, high-quality, population-based, time-series data on global biodiversity?
- How are human populations moving and developing, and what effects do these shifts and their accompanying infrastructure developments have on biodiversity?
- How do we understand the impacts of variable environmental forcing and climate change on biodiversity?
- What genetically and structurally unique characteristics exist that will provide new medicines, products, processes, and designs?

## Climate

The climate SBA addresses the observational needs of a wide variety of climate-related activities, including modeling/projecting, mitigation, adaptation planning, and risk assessment. Climate change has wide-ranging impacts on human health, ecosystem dynamics, commerce, ocean acidification, water availability, and water quality. There is a need for long-term, consistent measurements of baseline climate data for climate monitoring, change prediction, and science, to understand critical aspects of the climate signal or fundamental Earth system processes. In addition, observation and research are needed to support regional and local adaptive-management strategies, and to inform and evaluate greenhouse-gas-mitigation policies. Climate observations for these and other purposes can include atmospheric, oceanic, and land observations at scales ranging from a watershed to regional to global. An appropriate mix of platforms is necessary to provide needed observations at these scales. Key questions include the following:

- What is the contribution of specific observing-system capability to the confidence of climate prediction and projections, separately and collectively?
- How do trends in human systems (such as human populations and consumption changes) affect climate?

- How can we measure, track, and verify greenhouse-gas emissions reliably enough to raise the quality of "bottom-up" reporting of greenhouse gas sources and sinks?
- How will the dynamics of ecological carbon fixation, sequestration, and release change as carbon dioxide becomes more abundant?
- How do air-pollution-mitigation strategies, which may be focused on ozone and aerosols, affect global climate change, weather predictions, and air-quality concerns on regional and global scales?
- How do regional and global climate changes affect air quality?
- What changes in cloud cover, Earth's albedo, and ocean heat uptake affect the overall heat budget and warming of the planet?
- What are the probability and the likely effects of major loss of the major ice sheets? How quickly is sea level rising on average, regionally, and near low-lying population centers and sensitive ecosystems? Can we understand this better by monitoring ice-sheet-melting dynamics, mass change, and glacial hydrology?
- How do climate variations affect the intensity and frequency of smaller scale weather phenomena? To what extent do mesoscale weather phenomena and processes affect the climate and therefore need to be represented in climate models?
- How will the manner, seasonality, and regional distribution of precipitation—not just the total amount of precipitation—change with climate change? How can regional adaptation planning related to changes in water supply, farmland irrigation, and ecosystem shifts be improved through monitoring of precipitation amounts, snowpack changes, storm intensity, and other metrics?
- How can we address environmental stewardship needs in the Arctic Ocean and adjacent coastal areas in the face of climate and environmental changes?
- How does the thawing of onshore and offshore permafrost and the sublimation of coastal and offshore gas hydrates contribute to the release of $CO_2$ and methane into the atmosphere?
- How will the rate at which the ocean stores excess heat caused by climate change be modified as elements of the climate system evolve?
- What is the extent of the urban-heat-island effect in cities, and what characteristics of cities contribute to, or could mitigate, this effect?
- How will climate change influence living marine resources and marine ecosystems, and how can we mitigate those impacts?
- How are the extremes of climate changing? Are we able to measure them, and if so, with what confidence?

## Disasters

In the disasters area, societal benefits accrue from Earth observations used to monitor, predict, mitigate, respond to, assess the risk of, and provide early warning of events, including natural disasters resulting from earthquakes, landslides, droughts, coastal inundation, heat waves, tsunamis, tornadoes, winter storms, floods, wildfires, volcanic eruptions, tropical cyclones, and geomagnetic storms driven by space weather disturbances; as well as disasters that are at least partly human-induced, such as oil spills and other pollution events. The NSTC Subcommittee on Disaster Reduction has identified four key characteristics of disaster-resilient communities: (1) relevant hazards are recognized and understood; (2) communities at risk know when a hazard event is imminent; (3) individuals at risk are safe from hazards in their homes and places of work; and (4) communities experience minimum disruption to life and economy after a hazard event has passed. Changing the patterns of where we live, build businesses, and locate infrastructure could be the best option in terms of eliminating the risks communities face. Monitoring change (e.g., the Coastal Change Analysis Program) can help us understand where we are creating changes that put more people and economies at risk. All these characteristics can be achieved in whole or in part through enhanced or real-time Earth observations that embody systematic measurement programs to provide the capability to quantify the magnitude and impact of disasters through modeling and simulation. Key questions include the following:

- How are extreme events likely to change with changing atmospheric temperature, humidity, aerosol content, and wind patterns?
- Where are major fault systems nearing the release of stress caused by strong earthquakes, and where might associated landslides or tsunamis occur as a result? How rapidly can we characterize large earthquakes, including their tsunami potential?
- How do vulnerable populations and critical infrastructure map onto earthquake, flood, fire, landslide, and volcanic-eruption risks? Where (in real time) are important equipment and supply assets and vulnerabilities, as well as human assets?
- Where are areas with fuel loads or fuel continuity with high fire risk? How do we monitor fuels and local weather conditions at the forest level to improve our pre-fire forecasts and active fire-progression models?
- How do we detect and report new fire starts and provide active fire characterization (active fire fronts, hot spots, and dynamic fire-behavior reporting) for large fires that threaten lives, human health, ecosystems, and infrastructure?
- During preparation for major weather events, what are the likely impact, extent, timing, and intensity of events? How can we support protective measures against severe weather, such as taking shelter during tornado warnings, preparation for anticipated heavy snow, evacuation of coastal areas under hurricane threat, and rerouting aircraft to avoid severe weather?
- What are the most effective methods for sharing this information with intended audiences? How can it be most effectively coupled with existing applicable science-based information, in a format that is useful to the intended audience?

- During disaster response, what are the real-time extent, severity, and expected changes in flooding, fires, structural damage, etc.? What other potential hazards can be anticipated from leaking fuel tanks, downed power lines, washed-out roads, etc.?
- During disaster response, how can we accurately quantify the impacts and implement conservation and economic measures to minimize long-term impacts on the environment and economy?
- How can we link health databases with real-time monitoring and prospective assessment of weather, climate, geospatial, and exposure data to characterize the health impacts of extreme weather events?
- How can we better monitor and predict geomagnetic storms to mitigate the impact on electric power grids, corrosion of oil and gas pipelines, disruption of communication and navigation satellites, and damage to spacecraft?
- How do we better image changes in the landscape—primarily topographic, visual, and thermal—that will aid in more accurate forecasts, detection, and characterization of volcanic activity? How can we more accurately track long-lived volcanic ash and aerosol clouds that affect global aviation and cause health risks in populated areas threatened by ash clouds? How can we better calibrate satellite-based measurements with ground-based observations?
- How can we use historical records of disaster occurrences within regions to better determine rebuilding requirements, change of infrastructure, need for water catchment systems above ground and underground, and crop failures?
- How do we assess impact on, and forecast recovery of, biological communities damaged or affected by disasters (e.g., hurricanes and oil spills)?

## Terrestrial and Freshwater Ecosystems

In the area of terrestrial and freshwater ecosystems, societal benefits accrue from observations that enable ecological forecasting, such as the prediction of the effects of biological, chemical, physical, and human-induced pressures on ecosystems and the role of climate on ecosystems. Earth observations in this area help identify cause-effect relationships that can help managers mitigate and monitor ecosystem and climate changes, mitigate ecosystem impacts through ecosystem forecasts, and practice adaptive management. The SBA includes forests, watersheds, tundra, inland water, islands, and archipelagoes. This SBA focuses on terrestrial ecosystems. Coastal and marine ecosystems are included in the oceans and coastal resources SBA. Key questions include the following:

- Where are native and un-fragmented plant communities for grassland/shrub land/savanna, riparian, and forest cover types? Where are populations of ecologically unique endemic species and communities that are of management concern?
- What biophysical settings are necessary for the reestablishment of communities of concern? What areas have high potential to restore or reconnect endemic species populations?
- How can ecosystem-based management be facilitated through monitoring of population dynamics, migratory patterns, climate and weather forcings, and hydrology? How is the quantitative evaluation of ecosystem-nutrient dynamics affected by atmospheric dust and other aerosols?

- How is the range of the boreal (subarctic) forest likely to shift due to temperature and precipitation changes?
- How can we quantify and monitor ecosystem services at local and regional scales?
- What are the area and composition of urban and suburban landscapes, and how are these changing? What are the impacts of recent urban and suburban land-use changes on the environment, including effects on wildlife habitat, watersheds, and the water and carbon cycle?
- What are the environmental, social, and economic effects of proposed urban- or energy-development decisions under various policy scenarios and external drivers, including disasters?
- How can we monitor, authenticate, certify, monetize, and trade carbon flows from critical biosphere systems (e.g., global rainforests) at the regional or local level?
- In what ways can soil dynamics, including moisture, decomposition rate, and formation rate, affect large-scale patterns in vegetation and other global ecological processes?

## Energy and Mineral Resources

In the area of energy and mineral resources, societal benefits accrue from observations related to fossil-fuel extraction and production; renewable energy generation (including hydropower, wind power, bioenergy, solar power, and geothermal power); energy transportation and transmission; and availability and sustainability of critical mineral resources necessary for energy technologies, economic development, defense, and future innovation. Data needs are often application-specific. For example, Landsat and ASTER radiometric data are necessary to identify minerals and alteration associated with critical resources such as rare earth elements (REE), wind speed is a critical observation set for wind turbines, insolation and cloud-cover prediction are important for solar-energy, and surface water location and volume are critical to many energy- and resource-production industries—from copper and gold, to coal and nuclear to hydropower. In all cases, a goal is to enable planners and managers to predict 20-year trends with the confidence necessary to make utility-scale investments and land use planning decisions, based on data continuity and coverage. Key questions include the following:

- What is the distribution of alteration mineralogy associated with undiscovered resources such as the strategic minerals necessary for economic development, defense, and future technology?
- How will surface-water availability change over the time scale of supporting infrastructures, facilities, and technologies established for resource extraction and fossil fuel, hydropower and nuclear power production (50+ years)?
- How do atmospheric and topographic effects commonly seen in the United States affect local wind-energy potential? Can we generate reference data sets that enable the development and validation of reliable site-scale wind models?
- What is the energy potential of offshore winds? How can we bridge the gap between ocean and coastal characterizations, since remote sensing platforms on satellites offer invaluable information on the surface winds over the ocean but have limitations in the coastal zone?

- What solar-energy resources are likely to be available within a 3-hour time frame (to enable load balancing), on a 12- to 72-hour time frame (to enable forecasting), and on a seasonal-to-interannual time frame (to enable utility planning)?
- What are the cumulative environmental impacts of large-scale resource extraction and renewable-energy deployment in the United States? What monitoring protocols are necessary to enable regional-scale siting and adaptive management of energy and ecosystem resources (both terrestrial and oceanic)?
- What are the land-use and other environmental impacts of bioenergy programs and policies globally? How are land-use and land-cover changing around the world, and what are the bioenergy-related driving forces behind those changes?
- What are the spatial and temporal variation patterns in ocean waves, currents, and tides? Can we harness the energy they provide?
- What are the environmental impacts of mineral resource and fossil-fuel extraction, transportation, and use?
- How much energy is used in urban metabolism (the flows of the materials and energy within cities), and what are the types and distribution of energy sources for urban and industrial energy emissions?
- How does urban and industrial energy use affect air temperature and water temperatures, aerosol loading, atmospheric chemistry, and human health?

## Human Health

The health area includes societal benefits from the observation of air quality, aeroallergens, and infectious diseases, among other factors. Understanding aeroallergens and air quality depends heavily on atmospheric measurements, while infectious disease has an important waterborne component. Accelerating climate change may exacerbate a number of these stressors, including the spread of disease, toxins, and contaminants. Earth observations can serve as indicators and early-warning systems for food security, water and soil quality and quantity, harmful algal blooms and seafood contamination, air quality, and other major contributors to human health. These and other indicators can be combined with socioeconomic data and infrastructural indicators to provide a rich data set related to human health and well-being. Key questions include the following:

- How does economic development in underdeveloped countries affect changes in land and water use that affect the production of land, water, and air pollutants? How are those pollutants transported on the local scale and across oceans and continents? How are those pollutants transformed during the transport process?
- How do we most effectively maintain awareness of potential changes in insect-, mammal-, and protozoan-borne disease vectors in proximity to vulnerable human populations?

- How do we most efficiently monitor air quality and air-pollution exposures and understand the emissions sources and the physical and chemical atmospheric processes that determine those exposures?
- How do we monitor the influence of climate change on, and what measurements do we need to monitor, human-health stressors such as air quality, aeroallergens, aerosolized pathogens, dust burdens, and other pollutants directly linked to asthma and other human health effects?
- What factors initiate harmful algal blooms and bacterial proliferations? How do temperature change, shifts in rainfall patterns, and other climate-associated factors affect their distribution, occurrence, and severity?
- How can data from new biosensors for pathogens, contaminants, harmful algal blooms, and toxins be connected with data from ocean and coastal observing systems and new epidemiological studies of human disease to better protect the public from ocean-borne health threats?
- How can data from observing the ocean ecosystems and biodiversity be used to develop products and biological models to enhance human well-being?

## Ocean and Coastal Resources and Ecosystems

The ocean and coastal resources SBA focuses on the characteristics of, and risks to, ocean, coastal, and Great Lakes populations and ecosystems. Global, regional, and local trends in natural processes and human demands on coastal and ocean ecosystems may affect the ability of these ecosystems to support commerce, living resources, recreation, and habitation. Coastal communities are at risk from coastal hazards, development, and urbanization. The multiple stressors on coastal and ocean ecosystems, including population growth, land use, loss of biodiversity, habitat degradation, pollution, sea-level rise, and natural processes, lead to health threats to human and marine life. Observations are needed to understand interactions between coastal, marine, and terrestrial systems across the land-sea interface. Key questions include the following:

- How can we sustainably manage and monitor coastal and ocean ecosystems, particularly those that are subject to intense human harvesting?
- What air and land-based environmental contaminants are present in coastal waters?
- How is ocean chemistry changing over time (e.g., acidification due to rising $CO2$ or other causes)?
- How can we predict the future extent of ocean acidification and its long-term ecological consequences, including the capability of marine organisms to adapt, and the impacts on sustainability of harvested living resources?
- How can we ensure that the U.S. ocean, coastal, and Great Lakes communities are environmentally and economically sustainable against the backdrop of natural and man-made hazards, pollution, declining ocean and coastal ecosystems, climate change, population growth, and competing uses?
- How can we ensure that goods and commerce will flow safely and effectively to and from the United States?

- How do we monitor and improve the safety of seafood in the face of natural- and human-mediated contamination?
- Which marine fish stocks are overexploited, and what are the trends in resource abundance and distribution?
- How can we strengthen the resilience of coastal communities and marine and Great Lakes environments and their abilities to adapt to climate change-impacts and ocean acidification?
- What biophysical settings are necessary for the reestablishment of communities of concern? What areas have high potential to restore or reconnect endemic species populations?
- How can monitoring population dynamics, migratory patterns, climate and weather forcings, and hydrology aid ecosystem-based management?
- How can we quantify and monitor ecosystem services at local and regional scales?
- How do human activities (e.g., resource utilization, structures, disturbances, discharges, and runoff) affect ocean and coastal ecosystems?
- What environmental factors and human activities are affecting and limiting the populations of endangered and threatened species?
- How can conservation efforts and marine resources habitat restoration be more effective or enhanced?

## Space Weather

The space weather SBA focuses attention on improving understanding of the possible impacts of space weather phenomena—magnetic disturbances of the upper atmosphere and near-Earth space caused by solar activity. These currents can interfere with high-frequency (HF) radio communications, navigation signals from Global Positioning System (GPS) satellites, power grid systems, and other technological systems. These events could result in signal degradation or system loss, which could severely impact modern communication technologies. This SBA aims to improve current space weather assessment and prediction mechanisms in order to prevent and mitigate potential impacts. Key questions include the following:

- What are the potential economic and societal implications of a disruption to critical technological systems by severe space weather activity?
- What vulnerabilities do current technological systems have to space weather?
- How may future technologies be vulnerable to space weather?
- What impacts would a severe geomagnetic storm have on the U.S. electric power grid?
- What would be the immediate implications of sudden losses on the U.S. electrical grid due to a severe geomagnetic storm?
- How quickly could capabilities be restored to electrical grids in the event of a geomagnetic caused outage?

- How robust are the current capabilities to predict sudden geomagnetic storms?
- Are the current operational procedures during the event of a large storm adequate and up-to-date?
- What are the capabilities of current and planned surveillance systems?
- Currently what back-up systems are planned and implemented to support GPS signals and codes?
- How can GPS receiver technology be improved to remove ionospheric errors caused by interferences?
- What back up navigation systems are available that are independent of GPS and how do their capabilities compare to GPS?
- What would be the security, economic, and societal impacts of discrete or complete loss of satellite communication?
- What space weather measurement missions are currently planned or underway?
- What efforts can be made to gain more accurate space weather data, modeling, and space weather forecasts?
- How could space weather events impact the originally predicted lifetime of space technology systems?

## Transportation

The transportation SBA encompasses the societal benefits of improving the safety and efficiency of all modes of transportation, particularly as they relate to impacts from weather events. Transportation is a primary beneficiary of improved mesoscale weather observations since the impact of weather on modes of transportation can be significant. Severe weather can compromise the safety of transit but also accumulate traffic delays which result in sustained economic loss. Additionally, damage to public transportation infrastructure could be mitigated through improved understanding and prediction of weather events. Key questions include the following:

- How can weather-related transportation crashes be reduced?
- How can weather-induced delays be mitigated to minimize economic loss?
- What pre-existing technologies can be employed to improve safety in transportation during severe weather?
- How far reaching are the economic impacts of weather-related delays in transportation?
- How can infrastructure damage caused by weather be reduced to save money and protect public property?
- How can delays to air-traffic due to weather be minimized?
- How can real-time observational weather data be applied to improve transportation safety?

- How can the environmental impacts and costs associated with chemical anti-icing and de-icing materials be minimized?
- Since track washouts can severely impact safety and cause large amounts of damage, how can this type of damage be prevented?
- How can port operations be optimized following weather damage?
- What improvements can be made to maintain and improve roadside meteorological observing stations?
- How can roadside data be utilized in real-time safety and traffic decisions?
- How can the reliability of individual state data be made less variable?
- How can sensor data be made more readily accessible by neighboring states, decision makers, and transportation consumers?
- What developments can be made to advance integrated observational systems and data management for surface transportation?
- How can observational data be individualized for the observational needs of each relevant mode of transportation (i.e., railroad needs versus air transport)?
- How can we most efficiently route air-traffic to avoid volcanic ash and sulfur dioxide?
- How can we optimize routing efficiency for both air and maritime transportation?
- How can we best route ships though ice fields?

## Water Resources

Societal benefits accrue from observations related to water-resource management, emergency management, tourism, and recreation. This area focuses on terrestrial hydrology, including surface water, groundwater, terrestrial hydrological forcings, water quality, and water use. Oceans and coastal margins are covered in the oceans and coastal resources SBA. Improved understanding and management of the water cycle has wide-ranging implications for food security, energy development, human health protection, and critical habitat protection. Key questions include the following:

- What is the sustainable yield of a given watershed? How have the characteristics and health of the watershed changed, on seasonal to decadal scales?
- Where will changes in water supply affect the viability of nuclear, hydroelectric, or innovative power generation?
- How are changing snowpack, rainfall, surface water, and groundwater affecting water-storage needs in the United States?
- How have water-usage patterns changed over time? How have those changes affected water quality and supplies?

- How do precipitation, temperature, evaporation, and other hydrologic processes influence water availability and quality?
- What are the transport and fate characteristics of chemicals, nutrients, sediments, pathogens, harmful algal blooms, toxins, and marine debris in waterways?
- To protect drinking-water intakes and reduce unnecessary and expensive beach closures, what systems and networks are needed to advance the rapid detection of contaminant plumes and pathogens in rivers and recreational waters?
- How are changes in evaporation, precipitation, soil moisture, and human water usage affecting the balance of the water cycle on local to regional scales?
- How can we better monitor water use by individuals in areas where there are water-rights conflicts, and how can we supply the prior and current consumption data required to negotiate interstate and international water compacts?
- How can we identify regions or countries where freshwater resources are becoming scarce, posing a potential threat to sociopolitical stability and food security?

## Weather

Societal benefits accrue from observations that support improved weather information, forecasting, and warning, including numerical weather prediction, nowcasting, and atmospheric-chemistry monitoring. Social and economic sectors ranging from agriculture to aviation are directly affected by changes in temperature, precipitation, winds, and other general weather properties. Improvement in data sets and predictive capacity can enable these and other industries to plan for and respond to weather with more confidence. The weather SBA cuts across several other SBAs. Long-term observations of weather changes are related to climate observations, and low-frequency/high-impact events are closely tied to the disasters SBA. Weather prediction to support renewable energy development is also connected to the energy SBA. Key questions include the following:

- How do improved weather forecasts affect regional economic decisions such as pre-positioning store items in anticipation of increased demands (e.g., snow shovels in advance of heavy winter storms, water and canned goods in preparation for tropical storms, or umbrellas during periods of heavy rain).
- How do improved weather forecasts support emergency managers in preparation for, or response to, developing weather conditions? For example, emergency managers may delay or cancel public events, call in additional snow plow operators, or lift high-occupancy-vehicle controls, in response to weather information tailored to their requirements.
- How do meteorological effects, including convection, turbulence, and clouds, affect transport of chemical compounds and atmospheric chemistry?
- In what ways do weather and climate services need to be tailored to urban environments? How can we provide the level of resolution and surface specificity necessary to produce forecasts on the urban scale?

- How can we improve mesoscale predictive capabilities (tens to hundreds of kilometers) to tailor weather impacts to specific local areas and increase the effectiveness of preparation?
- How do convection, chemical transport, and winter precipitation types evolve throughout the lowest 2 to 3 kilometers of the atmosphere?
- In what ways do precipitation patterns vary on the mesoscale? Can understanding this variability enable quantitative precipitation forecasts to enable more effective planning and response to weather events?
- How can we reduce loss of life and property, and minimize disruption from high-impact weather events?
- How do soil moisture and evaporation patterns on the landscape affect drought persistence (precipitation recycling)?

## Reference Measurements

Internationally recognized references and measurement standards are the foundation upon which all Earth-observation data and analyses rest. From these are derived the range of fundamental reference measurements critical to Earth observations. These include, but are not limited to, geodesy (measurement of Earth's shape and gravitational field), bathymetry (the study of the depth of oceans and lakes), topography (the measurement of land elevation), and geolocation (precise time and global positioning). These reference measurements, among others, are the foundation on which all Earth-observation data and analysis rest. It is critical to evaluate the requirements and coverage of reference measurements in any comprehensive prioritization of Earth observation needs, taking into account ground-truths when possible. In addition, overlap between congruent satellite missions should be preserved wherever possible, to ensure inter-calibration and long-term continuity/comparability of record.

# Appendix C: Interdependencies and Partnerships

The Nation's Earth-observing requirements are met through a combination of systems, including those that are entirely owned and operated by the Federal Government as well as "extramural" systems sustained by a complex patchwork of funding arrangements from both Federal and non-Federal sources. In many cases, Federal mission-driven agencies have become reliant on data from extramural systems for their operations. Often these are long-term, time-series data needed to support scientific understanding of climate change. Funding streams for extramural Earth observation systems are often interconnected, requiring the perpetual agreement of all parties that funding not be arbitrarily withdrawn. Despite best efforts, the stability of even the most important of these systems is routinely challenged by threats to their partial funding arrangements, from both Federal and non-Federal partners. While greater fiscal stability is needed in this domain, Federal agencies and partner entities have also worked to achieve substantial cost savings. USGEO is committed to tracking such efforts and highlighting the best arrangements to apply best practices and lessons learned.

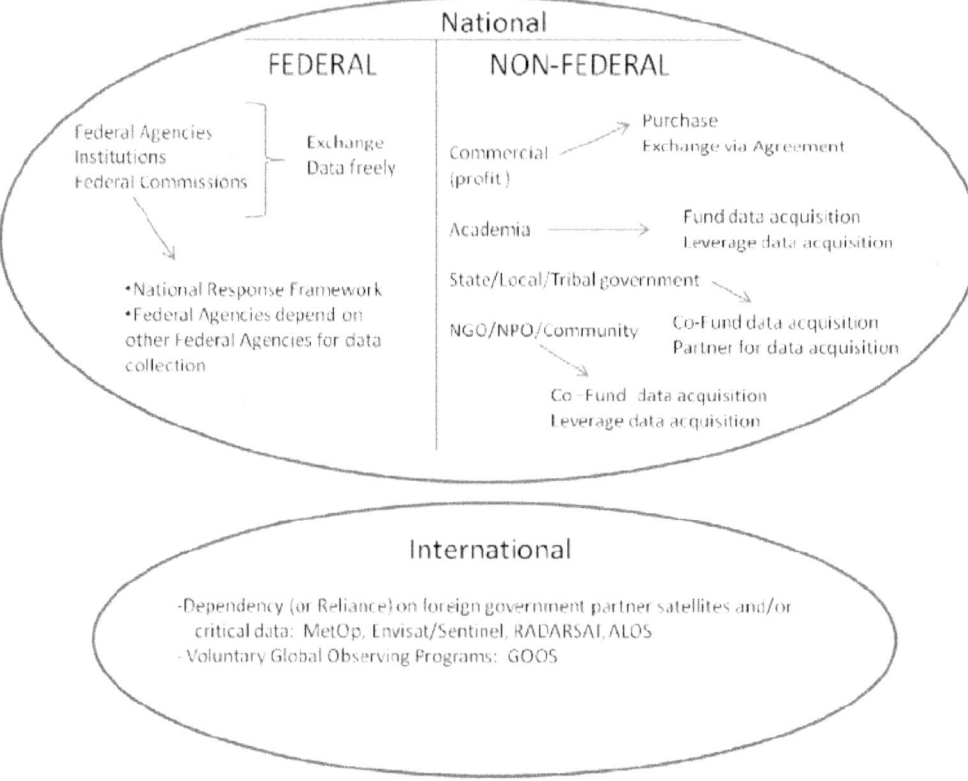

Figure 3: Relationships between Federal, non-Federal, and international stakeholders

# Appendix D: Data Principles and Definitions

## D.1. Data Principles

- **Full and Open Access** This National Strategy adheres to the principle that access to data-managed or paid for using Federal funds should be open to the public as soon as possible after collection, in a nondiscriminatory manner, and generally free of charge. This National Strategy respects the "presumption of openness" called for in 2009 Open Government Directive. Full, open, and timely sharing and exchange of data, products, and services will through machine-readable formats and APIs (Application Programing Interfaces) enable users to effectively and rapidly transform data into useful information for society. The timeliness, accessibility, and cost may not be the same in all cases (e.g., for routine, ongoing observations by automated sensors versus sporadic, labor-intensive data collection) but exceptions to this principle should be rare and explicitly justified on a case-by-case basis. For example, access to certain fishery-dependent data (observers, location of catch, and effort) are subject to confidentiality requirements that may affect the circumstances of their release.

- **Timeliness** Data should be made publicly available with minimum time delay after capture. Data processing, quality control, and assurance processes should be automated, whenever possible, to minimize delays. In limited circumstances, some scientific investigations may permit a temporary data hold before distribution.
- **Non-discrimination** Data should be made publicly available in a platform-agnostic manner to the widest community possible. Earth observations should be distributed in a way that does not unfairly hinder access to that data on any basis unless a specific exemption has been granted. Possible exceptions to open access include data whose public dissemination is prohibited by law (e.g., personally identifiable or proprietary information), international agreements, or for reasons of national security (e.g., classified information).
- **Minimum Cost** Data should be made available free of charge to the greatest extent possible. Whenever possible, data should be made available and accessible online via web services or other Internet-based mechanisms. Agencies may set user charges in a manner consistent with OMB Circular A-130.

These principles are exemplified by NASA's Earth Science data policy, which was almost universally "free-of-charge" even before the majority of NASA's data was available and accessible online. This has been long recognized at NASA as a key factor in the wide use of these data by stakeholder communities. Additionally, some programs, notably Landsat, were originally required to charge for data in an effort to recoup operations costs. Since USGS made the Landsat archives available free of charge over the Internet, public use of the data has dramatically increased.

- **Preservation**

  Earth observations are not reproducible after the moment of measurement has passed, and are often acquired using costly technologies, including satellites, advanced sensors, and open-ocean buoys. Therefore, these observations should be managed as agency and national assets. This means they should be preserved for future use and protected from unintended or malicious modification. The data should not merely be preserved as-is but should be made "durable." Some data deemed not to have long-term usefulness may not merit preservation; however, the decision not to preserve should be a conscious one rather than an accidental failure to preserve. NOAA's "Procedure for Scientific Records Appraisal and Archive Approval: Guide for Data Managers"[26] provides an example of agency-level guidance in this appendix.

- **Information Quality**

  Earth-observation data and ancillary information should be of known quality, meaning that they are fit for their intended use in operational missions and for planning. There may be times, however, when data must be distributed before quality control and documentation have been completed. For example, during the Deepwater Horizon oil spill in the Gulf of Mexico the responding agencies at times needed to share raw data immediately among personnel who had the expert knowledge to recognize and account for the limitations associated with those data. When data and web services are provided on an as-needed basis, quality parameters and uncertainties should be explained and clearly communicated to users. Quality control is discussed in more detail as part of Appendix D.3.

- **Ease of Use**

  To encourage the broadest possible use of Earth observations, users should be able to find the data easily. The data should be made available and accessible online via web services or other Internet-based mechanisms, rather than by shipping physical media or by establishing dedicated or proprietary linkages. These services should comply with non-proprietary, interoperability specifications for geospatial data. Where possible, Data should be offered in formats that are known to work with a broad range of scientific or decision-support tools. Common vocabularies, semantics, and data models should be employed. Feedback from users should be gathered and used to develop usability improvements. Users should be able to unambiguously cite datasets, both for later reuse and to provide credit and traceability to the originator.

---

[26] National Oceanic and Atmospheric Administration, *NOAA Procedure for Scientific Records Appraisal and Archive Approval: Guide for Data Managers: Guide for Data Managers*, 2008, www.ngdc.noaa.gov/wiki/images/0/0b/NOAA_Procedure_document_final.pdf.

## D.2 Metadata

Metadata provide information about data provenance, descriptive attributes, quality, accuracy, maturity, or the underlying structure in which data are stored. Metadata support interoperability with other systems, archives, and databases to facilitate data discovery and sharing, and are critical for documenting and preserving agencies' data assets. Reliable metadata, structured in a standardized manner, are essential to ensuring that data are used appropriately, and that any resulting analysis is credible.

The core metadata standards for national data are the FGDC Content Standard for Digital Geospatial Metadata and the International Organization for Standardization (ISO) standards in ISO 19115 (content) and ISO/TS 19139 (XML schema).

Certain types of metadata, such as a field-level dictionaries, documentation of units of measure, or coordinate reference system coordinates, are indispensable to any use or reuse of data and, therefore, must be collected and supported by discovery. Efforts should focus on creating a common baseline for metadata to achieve increased interoperability while enabling agencies to build more specific requirements on top of the baseline for individual data sets. Further, access must be incorporated into protocols to preserve the utility of the data. Additional descriptive metadata may include information that helps contextualize data, such as descriptions of measurements or analytic techniques, and are essential to their reuse beyond their original purpose. Inclusion of a data dictionary or schema as part of data metadata will help assure users to evaluate the data's fitness for use for a specific application domain. Metadata for data, products, and web services should be collected and provided using international standards to promote consistency and interoperability, support discovery through catalog search mechanisms, and support fitness-for-use assessments by potential end-users. Metadata should include as much information as possible regarding not only quality but source, lineage, responsible parties, and known limitations of the data.

## D.3. Data Lifecycle Activities

## Planning and Production Activities

Planning and production activities in the data life cycle comprise: requirements definition, planning, development, deployment, and operations. These include such tasks as assessing the need and requirements for a new observing system, planning how to meet those requirements, developing any necessary sensors, deploying the observing system, and operating and maintaining the observing system. We do not cover these topics in this annex, focusing instead on the management of actual data once observations are collected. Nevertheless, activities that occur later in the data life cycle may influence this phase. For example, a calibration error discovered through quality-control processes may lead to changes in the operating procedure.

*Data-Management Activities*

Data-management and usage activities in the data life cycle include:

- **Data Collection and Processing**

   These activities refer to the initial steps of receiving data from an Earth-observing sensor (or running a numerical model that generates data), ingesting the data into the initial storage location (which may not be the final archival site), and performing the processing necessary to transform raw data from the sensor (which may include telemetry or other ancillary information) into usable data records.

- **Quality Control**

   Data quality standards are highly dependent on the nature of the data and the purpose for which they are used. Agencies should clearly and publicly document their data standards and the process by which those standards are applied to assess the quality of actual data. Agency data should be of known quality, which means that the result of the quality-control process, and a link to descriptions of the process and standard, are available in the data documentation.

   Quality-control (QC) tests should be applied to the data, including both automated QC in near-real-time and delayed-mode, human-assisted checks. Quality-assurance (QA) processes should be applied to provide validation that Earth-observation data meet, and continue to meet, their intended requirements throughout the Data Lifecycle. All QC and QA checks should be publicly described and peer-reviewed. The results of these checks should be included in metadata. All bad, suspect, and missing values should be flagged as such.

   Information quality is composed of three elements—utility, integrity, and objectivity (U.S. Department of Commerce, Section 515 Standards). Data quality will be ensured and established at levels appropriate to the nature and timeliness of the information to be disseminated. Utility means that disseminated information is useful to its intended users. Data integrity refers to security—information must be safeguarded from improper access, modification, or destruction, to a degree commensurate with the probability and magnitude of harm that could result from the loss, misuse, unauthorized access, or modification of such information. Objectivity ensures that information is accurate, reliable, and unbiased, and that information products are presented in an accurate, clear, complete, and unbiased manner.

   This framework, wherever possible, should follow the guidelines of the Data Quality Act, which directs the OMB to issue guidelines that "provide policy and procedural guidance to Federal Agencies for ensuring and maximizing the quality, objectivity, utility, and integrity of information (including statistical information) disseminated by Federal Agencies." These guidelines are designed so that agencies can incorporate the standards and procedures required by these guidelines into their existing information resources management and administrative practices rather than create new and potentially duplicative or contradictory processes. Agencies need only ensure that their own guidelines are consistent with OMB guidelines, and then ensure that their administrative mechanisms satisfy the standards and procedural requirements in the new agency guidelines. This assurance is a pre-requisite for agency postings to Data.gov, now a primary catalog for all government data, including Earth-observation data. Furthermore, this framework should follow the principles of the intergovernmental GEO "Quality Assurance Framework for Earth Observation" (QA4EO), which includes associated QA/QC information with data and datasets to support harmonization and interoperability, and enable reproducibility.

- **Documentation**

  Documentation activities produce metadata as defined in Annex D.2. Documentation may occur multiple times during the data lifecycle, and may be performed by a variety of systems and individuals. For example, basic information about the sensor system, location and time are available at the moment of data collection; subsequent quality control provides additional metadata; later analysis and use of the data may result in new or revised documentation. It is important that these documentation steps be performed at the appropriate times by qualified personnel, recorded in a standard fashion, and bundled or associated with the data.

- **Dissemination**

  Data should be made available and accessible online via web services or other Internet-based mechanisms, rather than by shipping physical media or by establishing dedicated or proprietary linkages. Immediate access to online data is preferable to delayed access via ordering services to near-line or off-line data. This goal is not always achievable for high-volume data collections, in which case agencies should carefully consider and optimize caching algorithms based on usage tracking to maximize the likelihood of popular data being online.

  Dissemination may be accomplished in a "pull" mode, whereby users request data they desire on an ad hoc or periodic basis, or in a "push" mode whereby the data provider sends data to recipients on a subscriptions basis.

  Agencies should consider distributed virtual storage in the Internet "cloud," especially for popular datasets, which can be helpful in reducing storage and bandwidth requirements in their data centers. See the U.S. Chief Information Officer's 25 Point Implementation Plan to Reform Federal Information Technology Management (2010) for more on this topic.

  Data should be offered in formats that are known to work with a broad range of scientific or decision-support tools. Common vocabularies, semantics, and data models should be employed.

- **Cataloging**

  "Cataloging" is used here in a general sense to refer to all mechanisms established by data providers through which users are able to find the data they need. The word "discovery" is employed to refer to the user's act of finding data. Cataloging thus enables discovery.

  Federal agencies should seek to ensure that Earth observations are readily accessible to the diverse community of domestic and international information providers and users. Data collected for a particular purpose can only be reused for novel purposes if those unanticipated users are able to discover the data. Furthermore, as science progresses and policy debates sharpen, the discussion of ideas and dissemination of findings depends critically on the ability to find relevant

  data outside of one's agency or normal information community. For example, it is often useful to combine data from Earth observation sensors with socio-economic analyses or political and cultural assessments to perform impact and options studies.

  Cataloging methods include establishing formal standards-based catalog services, building thematic or agency-specific portals, enabling commercial search engines to index data holdings, and implementing emerging techniques such as feeds, self-advertising data, and casting. Catalog Services are the current dominant mechanism for the discovery of geospatial data and information sources and have been crucial for those who seek to understand or apply Earth-observation data and information. Accordingly, interoperable cataloging technologies for information resources and data holdings comprise a foundational requirement of the Data-Management Framework.

- **Preservation and Stewardship**

  Long-term data durability requires both preservation (ensuring the data are stored and protected from loss) and stewardship (ensuring the data continue to be accessible, e.g., by migrating to new storage technologies) and are updated, annotated, or replaced when there are changes or corrections.

  A major challenge to long-term preservation of data is the ability of the hosting agency to guarantee the authenticity and quality of its digital holdings over time. Therefore, data archives will include easily accessible information about data holdings, data structures, and data products and will include quality assessments and supporting information for efficient data discovery and retrieval. Federal Earth observation archives will adhere to data archiving guidelines that meet or exceed current national and international standards.

- **Usage Tracking**

  Usage tracking refers to the ability of the agency to measure whether their data are actually being used. Crude estimates can be made by counting data requests or data-transmission volumes from Internet servers. Such statistics, however, do not reveal (1) whether data that were obtained were actually used; (2) if the data were used, whether they were helpful or had an impact; or (3) whether the initial recipient redistributed the data to other users.

  More sophisticated means of assessing usage—while preserving the anonymity of users—are desirable. To enable better usage tracking, data should be made available through application programming interfaces (APIs); it may be possible to capture more insightful information about how data and web services are being used.

- **Final Disposition**

  Agencies should establish a procedure to determine the final disposition of data. Not all data and derived products must be archived. Agencies should establish a process whereby an evaluation regarding what to archive is performed for each class of Earth observation. Ideally, because an observation cannot be repeated once the moment has passed, all observations should be retained, but trade-offs are possible. For example, perhaps derived products that most users have access to may adequately replace raw data and processing algorithms. Model-generated data, which are often quite voluminous, similarly pose the question of whether to archive the model outputs or merely the model code and initialization. Software algorithms and models do not require much storage space, but ensuring the ability to run the code in perpetuity may be difficult.

*Usage Activities*

Activities related to data usage in the data lifecycle comprise:

- **Discovery and Reception**

  Users must be able to find and access the data they want. These activities are enabled by the dissemination, cataloging, and documentation actions discussed above.

- **Analysis**

  "Analysis" includes such activities as a quick evaluation to assess the usefulness of a data set, including a data set among the factors leading to a decision, or an actual scientific analysis of the data in a research context. Such activities are only possible if the data have been well-documented and are of known quality.

- **Product Generation**

  Some uses of data involve creating new data products, such as by averaging, combining, differencing, interpolating, or assimilating data. These new products may themselves constitute a new source of data that merits its own life-cycle data-management process. Agencies are encouraged to relate the products they generate back to the original source data via appropriate documentation and catalog cross-referencing.

- **User Feedback**

  The design, implementation, and use of Earth-observing data systems and processes should take usability, defined by ISO as "the extent to which a product can be used by specified users to achieve specified goals with effectiveness, efficiency, and satisfaction in a specified context of use," into account as part of an integrated data-management life-cycle process. Data users should have a mechanism to provide feedback to the agency regarding ease of use, suspected quality issues, and other aspects of the data. Concerns should be evaluated through the lens of community standards by Federal agencies and by the relevant user groups that rely on Earth-observation data.

- **Citation**

  Citation refers to the ability to unambiguously reference a data set that was used as input to a model, a decision, or a scientific paper. This is a topic of ongoing interest that has not been solved. Workshops in 2011 included Geo-Data Informatics: Exploring the Life Cycle, Citation and Integration of Geo-Data[27] sponsored by the NSF and Developing Data Attribution and Citation Practices and Standards[28] sponsored by the National Academy of Sciences (NAS) Board on Research Data and Information (BRDI).

- **Tagging**

  Tagging refers to the ability to identify a data set as relevant to some event, phenomenon, purpose, program, or agency without needing to modify the original metadata. The ability to tag is essential because the current practices of (1) creating new catalogs and asking people to re-register a relevant subset of their data there or (2) asking people to add new metadata tags such that an external project can detect them (cf. GEOSS DataCORE) are not scalable because they require additional work and lead to the proliferation of duplicate data sets and metadata records. Existing examples of tagging today include the ability of Facebook users to tag individuals in a photo or of desktop photo-management software to tag all photos of "Italy" or "sunsets" without modifying either the file-level metadata or the folder hierarchy. Tagging relates to cataloging in the sense that tags are additional metadata associated with another metadata record.

---

[27] Geo-Data Informatics: Exploring the Life Cycle, Citation and Integration of Geo-Data (Broomfield, Colorado, March 2011), http://tw.rpi.edu/web/Workshop/Community/GeoData2011.

[28] Developing Data Attribution and Citation Practices and Standards (Berkeley, California, August 2011). http://sites.nationalacademies.org/PGA/brdi/PGA_064019.

- **Gap Analysis**

  Gap analysis refers to the determination by users that more data are needed. Such a determination influences the requirements-definition activity that is the start of a new data life cycle.

Some aspects of these activities are outside the scope of agency data management *per se*. Once users have obtained the data they seek, agencies may have little or no knowledge or control over how those data are used. Nevertheless, the ability to obtain and use data is a primary indicator of a good life-cycle data-management process, and information from or about users and their data-seeking experience can be a valuable tool as agencies seek to improve their data management processes.

# Annex A: National Earth Observations Task Force Formation

**Strengthening Federal Mechanisms for the**
**Coordination of Civilian Earth Observations**
*December 22, 2010*

## I.    The Value of Integrated Earth Observations

Each day, the scientific community collects millions of individual Earth observations, allowing us to examine, monitor, and model atmospheric composition, seismic activity, ecosystem health, weather patterns, and hundreds of other characteristics of our planet. Through these national investments in Earth observations, the U.S. government ensures that our Nation's decision makers, businesses, farmers, health care workers, and indeed all our citizens have the information they need to cope with weather-related and other environmental threats to human well-being.

The myriad of observations taken today vary widely in purpose and scope and are distributed among hundreds of programs under the purview of Federal agencies and other institutions and individuals. The Obama Administration recognizes that a coordinated approach is needed to cost-effectively sustain and build on the current set of Earth observations. Beyond coordination, there is a need to ensure that Earth observations are maintained and continued with diligence commensurate with their economic and environmental importance.

## II.    Congressional Direction

Section 702 of the NASA Authorization Act of 2010, signed into law on October 11, 2010, provides that the Director of the Office of Science and Technology Policy (OSTP) shall establish a mechanism to ensure greater coordination of civilian Earth observations. This should include the development of a strategic implementation plan that is updated at least every 3 years. The Director shall provide a report to Congress within 90 days of enactment on the implementation plan for this mechanism.

## III.    Planned OSTP Actions in Response to Congressional Direction

In proceeding to strengthen civilian coordination of Earth observations, OSTP, in collaboration with other offices within the Executive Office of the President (EOP) and federal agency representatives, will establish a National Task Force on Earth Observations to draft a National Strategy for Earth Observations. Among other elements, the National Strategy will consider:

a) A review of issues and options concerning the challenge of transferring civilian Earth observation measurement responsibilities from a demonstration agency to a long-term data acquisition agency. The strategy will examine critical decision points where research missions should be evaluated, possible criteria for determining whether a particular observational capability should be made operational, and recommendations for facilitating the transfer of meritorious research missions to operational use.

b) Criteria for prioritizing among observing systems as part of the budget process. The strategy will approach how best to measure Earth system parameters with a view toward optimizing and prioritizing the mix of satellite and *in situ* systems. In addition, the strategy will consider the nation's investment in satellite operations, data-management, and information-delivery systems as an integral part of the national observing system infrastructure. The strategy will build on the OSTP report released to Congress in September 2010, *Achieving and Sustaining Earth Observations: A Preliminary Plan Based on a Strategic Assessment by the U.S. Group on Earth Observations.* Once completed, the strategy will serve as standing guidance for preparation of agency Earth observation programming and budgets over time.

c) A strengthened national governance and coordination mechanism to support the implementation of the strategy and address its recommendations. The governance mechanism will evolve from the existing work and coordination efforts of the United States Group on Earth Observations (USGEO), a subcommittee of the National Science and Technology Council's Committee on Environment Natural Resources and Sustainability (CENRS). While acknowledging agency mission priorities and working with existing channels, the mechanism will be designed such that agencies are responsive to its guidance in the formulation of their budgets, and through it, the Office of Management and Budget (OMB) can enhance cross-agency integration of Earth observation budget priorities. The governance mechanism will also function as the national coordination point for interaction with the intergovernmental Group on Earth Observations (GEO) and other international activities and agreements relating to Earth observations. Further, the mechanism will draw upon the cross-agency efforts to implement the Open Government Directive and enhance Data.gov with more high-value data and data services.

The task force will be co-led by OSTP, the National Aeronautics and Space Administration (NASA), the National Oceanic and Atmospheric Administration (NOAA) of the Department of Commerce, and the United States Geological Survey (USGS) within the Department of Interior. Its membership will include the organizational, member-agency principals of the CENRS and senior officials from within the EOP appointed by the Assistant to the President for Science and Technology.

The task force will be established by February 2011 and complete its interim recommendations by May 2011. Following a full CENRS concurrence, the task force will submit its interim recommendations to the National Academies for a review and comment period not to exceed three months. The task force will revise the strategy based on comments from the National Academies, and the Administration will release the National Earth Observation Strategy based on those revisions.

## IV. Approach to a National Strategy for Earth Observations

Since early 2010, OSTP has consulted widely across Federal agencies to gather viewpoints on the best approach for developing a national strategy for Earth observation. From these consultations, OSTP concludes that:

1. Different agencies are usually responsible for research and operations, creating discontinuities in the way Earth observation assets (satellite, sensor, and measured) are developed, managed, operated, and funded. A sustained commitment to coordinated satellite system and sensor development is necessary to make effective use of taxpayer investments and avoid a loss of observing capability in the next decade.

2. Coordinated attention to *in situ* systems is needed.

3. The strategy must examine the process for appropriately prioritizing investments in the development of Earth observation applications, so that the nation can fully capitalize on its major Earth observation investments. The strategy must also allow for a critical level of research and experimentation to complement those investments made to fulfill user-driven needs.

4. The strategy must consider and address the observational needs of the US Global Change Research Program (USGCRP), the National Climate Assessment (NCA), the Interagency Climate Change Adaptation Task Force, the Climate Change Technology Program (CCTP), the Climate Roundtable on Climate Information and Services (RCIS), the National Ocean Council (NOC), and the Administration's other clean energy, environmental, and climate change mitigation efforts.

5. The strategy must support and build on the appropriate language and concepts in the National Space Policy, the Arctic Region Policy, and the National Policy for the Stewardship of the Ocean, Our Coasts, and the Great Lakes. The national strategy must also take account of the previous work of the USGEO strategic assessment, delivered in the OSTP September 2010 report to Congress on Earth observations. In addition, the national strategy should take account of the work of the Office of the Federal Coordinator for Meteorology (OFCM), as well as existing plans for Arctic observations, the U.S. Integrated Ocean Observing Systems (IOOS), agricultural, and other systems.

6. The strategy and governance mechanisms must support transparency and open government, the Open Government Directive, and leverage the evolving Data.gov infrastructure for delivery of data and data services.

## V. Conclusion

One of the primary functions of OSTP is to provide the leadership and needed coordination of national Earth observation activities. In assembling the National Task Force on Earth Observations, OSTP will bring together expertise from across the government, drawing from each agency's distinctive capacity, to construct the relationships and interactions among the agencies that will result in a program for Earth observations that contributes to both our national prosperity and our national security.

## VI. *Additional Background: GEO, USGEO, and the Visionary Frameworks of GEOSS and IEOS*

The concept of integrated Earth observations achieved international prominence in 2005 with the establishment of the intergovernmental GEO and its agreement to build a Global Earth Observation System of Systems (GEOSS) over 10 years. This concept has been endorsed and is currently being implemented by 85 governments, the European Commission, and 58 international organizations. The United States co-leads this international activity with China, the European Commission, and South Africa. GEOSS represents a grand vision for comprehensively observing the Earth system and integrating the data gathered from such observations into useful information for society.

Concurrent with the establishment of GEO, OSTP formed a working group on Earth observations under the National Science and Technology Council (NSTC), which published its *Strategic Plan for the U.S. Integrated Earth Observation System (IEOS)* in late 2005 as the U.S. national contribution to GEOSS. This working group was later re-constituted as USGEO, and is now a standing subcommittee of the CENRS. USGEO was chartered to begin implementing the U.S. IEOS and to serve as the national coordination mechanism for making input to GEOSS.

Since 2005, USGEO has released a number of important reports that clearly articulate those areas of opportunity that are ripe for national investment in Earth observation, and maintained a substantial U.S. engagement with the intergovernmental GEO. Most recently, USGEO conducted a strategic analysis of the nation's Earth observing requirements, resulting in a valuable list of 17 Earth system parameters and corresponding observing systems considered most essential for achieving the societal benefit areas identified in the IEOS plan. This analysis was the foundation of the OSTP report released to Congress in September 2010, as a first step toward a national strategy for Earth observations.

# Annex B: History of United States Global Change Research Program Data Principles

The data requirements for understanding global change were tabulated intensively by NASA Headquarters during the mid- to late-1980s, working with the broad Earth observation user community within and outside the U.S. Government. An early team called the Earth Observation System (EOS) Science and Mission Requirements' Working Group defined a suite of instruments for acquiring measurements of the Earth's atmosphere, surface, and interior from low Earth orbit; an information system to support scientific research; and a vigorous program of scientific research, stressing study of global-scale processes that shape and influence the Earth as a system. As a result, NASA's Earth Observation System Program was initiated in 1991.

At that time, NASA established a policy on the availability to the public of NASA-acquired Earth science and applications data. A major impetus of this new policy was the tenet that data would be made available to all users as soon as practicable after acquisition and without any period of exclusive access for any user group. The awareness of the importance of an open data policy grew out of unsatisfactory policies from the 1980s which allowed periods of exclusive use for certain user groups on key data sets.

Under the policy as originally conceived, the data would be provided to research users at a price not to exceed the marginal cost of reproduction and distribution. Later, in 1994, after consultation with the user community and study of current practices for NASA missions and at NOAA and USGS, NASA Headquarters waived this marginal cost of reproduction and distribution. NASA's aim was to promote the widest possible use of data, with a science-/user-driven system. The stated goal was not only to advance the science of remote sensing but to increase understanding of the Earth system. All research and applications demonstration users were asked to provide results for publication in scientific literature or as technical reports. Government-funded investigators were expected to make available research results, models, algorithms, and other supporting information to permit replication of research, consistent with U.S. law and policy.[29]

Congress mandated the United States Global Change Research Program in the Global Change Research Act of 1990 (Public Law 101-606). OSTP organized and worked with an interagency team composed of agency members of the USGCRP to create the data principles now commonly known as the "Bromley Principles," named for D. Allen Bromley, who was Science Advisor to President George H. W. Bush at the time. A statement of national policy, issued in July 1991, applied to all U.S. Government agencies, and established the framework within which agencies should work:

---

[29] The statements from NASA's current Earth Science Data Policy referred to in the body of this plan can be found at science.nasa.gov/earth-science/earth-science-data/data-information-policy/.

```
DATA MANAGEMENT FOR GLOBAL CHANGE RESEARCH POLICY STATEMENTS
July 1991

The overall purpose of these policy statements is to facilitate full and open access to quality data for global change
research. They were prepared in consonance with the goal of the U.S. Global Change Research Program and represent
the U.S. government's position on access to global change research data.
    •   The Global Change Research Program requires an early and continuing commitment to the establishment,
        maintenance, validation, description, accessibility, and distribution of high-quality, long-term data sets.
    •   Full and open sharing of the full suite of global data sets for all global change researchers is a fundamental
        objective.
    •   Preservation of all data needed for long-term global change research is required. For each and every global
        change data parameter, there should be at least one explicitly designated archive. Procedures and criteria for
        setting priorities for data acquisition, retention, and purging should be developed by participating agencies
        both nationally and internationally. A clearinghouse process should be established to prevent the purging and
        loss of important data sets.
    •   Data archives must include easily accessible information about the data holdings, including quality
        assessments, supporting ancillary information, and guidance and aids for locating and obtaining the data.
    •   National and international standards should be used to the greatest extent possible for media and for processing
        and communication of global data sets.
    •   Data should be provided at the lowest possible cost to global change researchers in the interest of full and open
        access to data. This cost should, as a first principle, be no more than the marginal cost of filling a specific user
        request. Agencies should act to streamline administrative arrangements for exchanging data among
        researchers.
    •   For those programs in which selected principal investigators have initial periods of exclusive data use, data
        should be made openly available as soon as they become widely useful. In each case, the funding agency
        should explicitly define the duration of any exclusive use period.
```

Source: Data Management for Global Change Research Policy Statements, U.S. Global Change Research Program, July 1991, www.gcrio.org/USGCRP/DataPolicy.html.

With these principles in mind, the United States also drove advances in international data policy in the early 1990s. NASA organized a group of partners to participate in the "International Earth Observing System," known as IEOS. The partners, including NASA, European Space Agency (ESA), European Organisation for the Exploitation of Meteorological Satellites (EUMETSAT), NOAA, Canadian Space Agency (CSA), National Association of State Departments of Agriculture (NASDA), and the Japanese Ministry of International Trade and Industry (MITI), were to work together to establish international data exchange principles for:

- NASA Earth Observing System
- ESA Polar Orbit Earth Observation Mission (POEM)
- NOAA POES series after NOAA-N
- NASA and NASDA's joint TRMM mission
- NASDA Advanced Earth Observation Satellite (ADEOS)

The U.S. civil space agencies NASA, NOAA, and USGS then used the Bromley Principles as background in the international Committee on Earth Observation Satellites (CEOS)[30] to develop an agreement by all CEOS members on Data Exchange Principles. These data exchange principles were meant to eventually cover the full range of remote sensing missions, focusing first on data exchange principles in support of global change research, and then continuing development of CEOS data principles beyond research use. At the Sixth CEOS Plenary meeting held in London in December 1992, the Resolution on Satellite Data Exchange Principles of Support of Global Change Research was adopted. These principles were developed at an ad hoc CEOS Data Policy Meeting hosted by CNES in Paris in October 1991, and they

---

[30] CEOS was formed in 1984 by the G-8 governments to foster cooperation among space agencies involved in Earth observing.

elaborated on the principles first adopted in 1991. The eventual CEOS Data Principles in Support of Operational Environmental Use for the Public Benefit were developed at an ad hoc Data Policy Meeting hosted by NOAA and NASA in Washington, DC, in April 1994. The principles were adopted at the eighth CEOS Plenary meeting held in Berlin in September 1994 and first published in the 1995 CEOS Yearbook.[31]

The first Earth Observation Summit convened in Washington, DC, in July 2003 and was attended by high-level officials from 33 countries, the European Commission, and 21 international organizations involved in Earth observations. The *Global Earth Observation System of Systems (GEOSS) 10-Year Implementation Plan*, published in February 2005, contains the GEOSS data-sharing principles (Section 6.1 Key principles).

These valuable and enduring U.S. data policies for Earth observation, and the concomitant exercises with our international partners, arose from widespread recognition of the importance of research and monitoring for global environmental understanding and sharing of data to support the public good. The observing capability to achieve these shared goals exceeds any single agency's or nation's resources. The commitment to timely, full and open, and unrestricted accessibility to data and information is shaped by the awareness of the complexity of the global environment and an appreciation for the value of observations in understanding and monitoring the Earth system.

---

[31] *Coordination for the next decade: 1995 CEOS yearbook.* Surrey, England: Smith System Engineering Ltd., 1995.

# Abbreviations Used

Abbreviations used in the National Strategy and Appendices are listed in alphabetical order.

**CENRS** Committee on Environment, Natural Resources, and Sustainability
**CEOS** Committee on Earth Observation Satellites
**CNES** Centre National d'Edutes Spatiales
**DMAC** Data Management and Communications
**DOI** Department of the Interior
**EOP** Executive Office of the President
**ESA** European Space Agency
**FGDC** Federal Geographic Data Committee
**GCIS** Global Change Information System
**GEO** Group on Earth Observations
**GEOSS** Global Earth Observation System of Systems
**GPS** Global Positioning System
**HabCam** Habitat Mapping Camera System
**IEOS** Integrated Earth Observation System
**ISO** International Organization for Standardization
**IOOS** Integrated Ocean Observing System
**JWG** NOAA Joint Working Group
**NASA** National Aeronautics and Space Administration
**NASDA** National Association of State Departments of Agriculture
**NEO** National Earth Observations
**NOAA** National Oceanic and Atmospheric Administration
**NOC** National Ocean Council
**NSF** National Science Foundation
**NSTC** National Science and Technology Council
**OFCM** Office of the Federal Coordinator for Meteorology
**OMB** Office of Management and Budget
**OSTP** Office of Science and Technology Policy
**PCAST** President's Council of Advisors on Science and Technology
**QA** Quality Assurance
**QC** Quality Control
**SBA** Societal Benefit Area
**SGCR** Subcommittee Global Change Research
**SOA** Service-oriented architecture
**SOST** Subcommittee on Ocean Science and Technology
**USGCRP** United States Global Change Research Program
**USGEO** United States Group on Earth Observations
**USGS** United States Geological Survey